# Day Walks
## Peak District

## 20 New Circular Routes

Design and production by Vertebrate Publishing, Sheffield
www.v-publishing.co.uk

# Day Walks in the Peak District

## 20 New Circular Routes

Written by
**Norman Taylor & Barry Pope**

# Day Walks in the PeakDistrict

## 20 New Circular Routes

**VG** Copyright © 2010 Vertebrate Graphics Ltd, Norman Taylor & Barry Pope

**VP** Published by **Vertebrate Publishing**

ISBN 978-1-906148-16-4

Cover photo by John Coefield: The view north up the Derwent Valley towards Win Hill, from Tumbling Hill, near Grindleford.

Back cover photo by Barry Pope: The descent from Crookhill Farm to Ladybower Reservoir.

All other photography as credited.

All maps reproduced by permission of Ordnance Survey on behalf of The Controller of Her Majesty's Stationery Office. © Crown Copyright. 100025218

Design by Nathan Ryder, production by Richard Griffin
www.v-graphics.co.uk

VERTEBRATE PUBLISHING

## Mixed Sources

Product group from well-managed forests and other controlled sources
www.fsc.org   Cert no. DNV-COC-000087
© 1996 Forest Stewardship Council

FSC

# Contents

## SECTION 1 – THE HIGH MOORS

## SECTION 2 – HILLS, TORS & EDGES

## SECTION 3 – LIMESTONE COUNTRY

## APPENDIX

LOOKING SOUTH FROM SHEEPWASH BANK (WALK 9)  PHOTO: JOHN COEFIELD

# Introduction

Set in the heart of England, the Peak District National Park attracts visitors from all over the world. They come to experience its dramatic moorland and crags, its spectacular gorges, caves and meandering rivers, and its fascinating archaeology and human settlement over thousands of years. This incredible variety of landscapes within a relatively small region reflects a complex geology and the natural forces of erosion upon this.

The moors in the north and to the east and west of the central area represent the Dark Peak, where the predominant underlying rock is a hard, gritty sandstone that becomes dark on exposure to the elements. Erosion here has produced the rocky 'tors', and earth movement has created long escarpments lined with gritstone crags. Where layers of shales are interspersed with bands of sandstone this has given rise to spectacular landslip features such as Mam Tor near Castleton and Alport Castles on Bleaklow.

In contrast, the central and southern Peak District is a region of rolling upland cut by craggy gorges. Here, the predominant underlying rock is a grey-white limestone. This is the White Peak. Erosion of the limestone by water has produced incredible cave systems with huge chambers. Mineral ores occurring within the limestone resulted in feverish mining activities in past centuries, this producing many man-made changes to the landscape.

Given that the wonderful countryside of the National Park is blessed with a fine network of public footpaths, bridleways and tracks, it is hardly surprising that it has attracted so much attention from writers of walking guides, ourselves included. Oddly, the middle distance walker has been less well catered for that those who enjoy shorter walks.

Thus, we embarked on the original Day Walks guide to the Peak District. It soon became obvious, however, that with so much potential for middle distance walks of quality, this was going to expand into a second volume. Here it is. As in the original Day Walks guide, the walks are evenly spread throughout the National Park and fall into one of three categories according to the terrain and predominant landscape encountered: The High Moor; Hills, Tors and Edges; and Limestone Country.

We hope you enjoy this new set of walks.

## Norman Taylor & Barry Pope

*Sadly, before publication of this second volume of Day Walks, my friend and accomplice in this venture,*
*Barry Pope, died. This book is dedicated to his memory.*
Norman Taylor

## Acknowledgements

The authors would like to thank the following people for their help:

Gess Boothby and his wife Wendy for testing *all* the walks in this guide, for checking route descriptions, and for suggestions for improvement; Ian (Hovis) and Jacqui Brown and Sarah Deakin for sampling some of the walks and offering critical feedback; and our wives Sue and Maureen for their continued support of the project.

## About the walks

All the walks are 'day' walks in the sense that they take 4 to 8 hours at an unhurried pace. They fall into three broad categories of terrain: walks on the high moors; walks on lower lying hills, tors and edges; walks in limestone country.

The **summary** and **route description** for each walk should be studied carefully before setting out on a walk. Together they describe the terrain involved, the amount of ascent and the level of navigation skills required.

## Walk times

The time given for each walk is on the generous side and based on a pace of around 4km per hour/2½ miles per hour, with time allowed for ascent and difficulty of terrain. There is some allowance for snack breaks and photo stops, but prolonged lunches should be added in.

## Navigation

For most walks in this guide, following the route description in combination with the route map provided should be sufficient. However it is recommended you carry with you the appropriate *Ordnance Survey Explorer* series map as a back up. These are shown for each walk. The Peak District is covered by two maps in the 1:25,000 series:

*Ordnance Survey Explorer OL1* (1:25,000) The Dark Peak
*Ordnance Survey Explorer OL24* (1:25,000) The White Peak

For moorland walks a reasonable level of map reading ability and competence in the use of a compass is strongly advised. If you possess a GPS (Global Positioning System) this can be a useful navigational aid in locating your position. However it is not a remedy for poor navigational skills.

## Mobile phones

Although there is a degree of mobile phone reception over much of the area covered by the 20 walks, don't count on it. Should you find yourself out of reception, be grateful to be temporarily free of the phone's tyranny, but bear in mind that you are also without its reassurance.

## Footpaths and rights of way

All the walks in this guide follow public rights of way or other routes with public access, including '*permitted*' or '*concession*' footpaths.

## Safety

It is strongly advised that appropriate footwear is used – walking boots designed to provide stability and security on uneven and slippery terrain. A waterproof, windproof jacket is essential and waterproof overtrousers or trousers are strongly recommended. Sufficient insulating clothing should also be worn or carried, that is appropriate to the type of walk planned and the time of year.

Trekking poles are a definite asset since they provide greater stability and security on steep ground or slippery footpaths, thereby lessening the chances of an accident resulting from difficult terrain.

On the high moor walks emergency rations should be carried in the event of the weather causing problems or an unplanned night out!

## Mountain Rescue

In case of accident or similar need requiring mountain rescue assistance, **dial 999** and ask for **POLICE – MOUNTAIN RESCUE**. Be prepared to give a 6-figure grid reference of your position in the case of a moorland location.

# The Countryside Code

## Be safe – plan ahead

Even when going out locally, it's best to get the latest information about where and when you can go; for example, your rights to go onto some areas of open land may be restricted while work is carried out, for safety reasons or during breeding seasons. Follow advice and local signs, and be prepared for the unexpected.

» Refer to up-to-date maps or guidebooks.
» You're responsible for your own safety and for others in your care, so be prepared for changes in weather and other events.
» There are many organisations offering specific advice on equipment and safety, or contact visitor information centres and libraries for a list of outdoor recreation groups.
» Check weather forecasts before you leave, and don't be afraid to turn back.
» Part of the appeal of the countryside is that you can get away from it all. You may not see anyone for hours and there are many places without clear mobile phone signals, so let someone else know where you're going and when you expect to return.

## Leave gates and property as you find them

Please respect the working life of the countryside, as our actions can affect people's livelihoods, our heritage, and the safety and welfare of animals and ourselves.

» A farmer will normally leave a gate closed to keep livestock in, but may sometimes leave it open so they can reach food and water. Leave gates as you find them or follow instructions on signs; if walking in a group, make sure the last person knows how to leave the gates.
» In fields where crops are growing, follow the paths wherever possible.

» Use gates and stiles wherever possible – climbing over walls, hedges and fences can damage them and increase the risk of farm animals escaping.

» Our heritage belongs to all of us – be careful not to disturb ruins and historic sites.

» Leave machinery and livestock alone – don't interfere with animals even if you think they're in distress. Try to alert the farmer instead.

## Protect plants and animals, and take your litter home
**We have a responsibility to protect our countryside now and for future generations, so make sure you don't harm animals, birds, plants or trees.**

» Litter and leftover food doesn't just spoil the beauty of the countryside, it can be dangerous to wildlife and farm animals and can spread disease – so take your litter home with you. Dropping litter and dumping rubbish are criminal offences.

» Discover the beauty of the natural environment and take special care not to damage, destroy or remove features such as rocks, plants and trees. They provide homes and food for wildlife, and add to everybody's enjoyment of the countryside.

» Wild animals and farm animals can behave unpredictably if you get too close, especially if they're with their young – so give them plenty of space.

» Fires can be as devastating to wildlife and habitats as they are to people and property – so be careful not to drop a match or smouldering cigarette at any time of the year. Sometimes, controlled fires are used to manage vegetation, particularly on heaths and moors between October and early April, so please check that a fire is not supervised before calling 999.

## Keep dogs under close control
**The countryside is a great place to exercise dogs, but it is owners' duty to make sure their dog is not a danger or nuisance to farm animals, wildlife or other people.**

» By law, you must control your dog so that it does not disturb or scare farm animals or wildlife. You must keep your dog on a short lead on most areas of open country and common land between 1 March and 31 July, and at all times near farm animals.

» You do not have to put your dog on a lead on public paths as long as it is under close control. But as a general rule, keep your dog on a lead if you cannot rely on its obedience. By law, farmers are entitled to destroy a dog that injures or worries their animals.

» If a farm animal chases you and your dog, it is safer to let your dog off the lead – don't risk getting hurt by trying to protect it.

» Take particular care that your dog doesn't scare sheep and lambs or wander where it might disturb birds that nest on the ground and other wildlife – eggs and young will soon die without protection from their parents.

» Everyone knows how unpleasant dog mess is and it can cause infections – so always clean up after your dog and get rid of the mess responsibly. Also make sure your dog is wormed regularly.

## Consider other people

**Showing consideration and respect for other people makes the countryside a pleasant environment for everyone – at home, at work and at leisure.**

» Busy traffic on small country roads can be unpleasant and dangerous to local people, visitors and wildlife – so slow down and, where possible, leave your vehicle at home, consider sharing lifts and use alternatives such as public transport or cycling. For public transport information, phone Traveline on 0871 200 2233.

» Respect the needs of local people – for example, don't block gateways, driveways or other entry points with your vehicle.

» By law, cyclists must give way to walkers and horse riders on bridleways.

» Keep out of the way when farm animals are being gathered or moved and follow directions from the farmer.

» Support the rural economy – for example, buy your supplies from local shops.

# How to use this book

This book should provide you with all of the information that you need for an enjoyable, trouble free and successful walk. The following tips should also be of help:

1. We strongly recommend that you invest in the maps listed above on page ix. These are essential even if you are familiar with the area – you may need to cut short the walk or take an alternative route.

**2**. Choose your route. Consider the time you have available and the abilities/level of experience of all of members your party – then read the safety section of this guide.

**3**. We recommend that you study the route description carefully before setting off. Cross-reference this to your OS map so that you've got a good sense of general orientation in case you need an escape route. Make sure that you are familiar with the symbols used on the maps.

**4**. Get out there and get walking!

## Maps, Descriptions, Distances

While every effort has been made to maintain accuracy within the maps and descriptions in this guide, we have had to process a vast amount of information and we are unable to guarantee that every single detail is correct.

Please exercise caution if a direction appears at odds with the route on the map. If in doubt, a comparison between the route, the description and a quick cross-reference to your OS map (along with a bit of common sense) should help ensure that you're on the right track. Note that distances have been measured off the map, and map distances rarely coincide 100% with distances on the ground. Please treat stated distances as a guideline only.

Ordnance Survey maps are the most commonly used, are easy to read and many people are happy using them. If you're not familiar with OS maps and are unsure of what the symbols mean, you can download a free OS 1:25,000 map legend from **www.v-outdoor.co.uk**

Here are a few of the symbols and abbreviations we use on the maps and in our directions:

 ROUTE STARTING POINT           SHORT CUT

**2** ROUTE MARKER           OPTIONAL ROUTE

**PB** = public bridleway; **PF** = public footpath; **GR** = grid reference: **KG** = kissing gate

## Km/mile conversion chart

### Metric to Imperial

| | | |
|---|---|---|
| 1 kilometre [km] | 1000 m | 0.6214 mile |
| 1 metre [m] | 100 cm | 1.0936 yd |
| 1 centimetre [cm] | 10 mm | 0.3937 in |
| 1 millimetre [mm] | | 0.03937 in |

### Imperial to Metric

| | | |
|---|---|---|
| 1 mile | 1760 yd | 1.6093 km |
| 1 yard [yd] | 3 ft | 0.9144 m |
| 1 foot [ft] | 12 in | 0.3048 m |
| 1 inch [in] | | 2.54 cm |

PHOTO: MAUREEN POPE

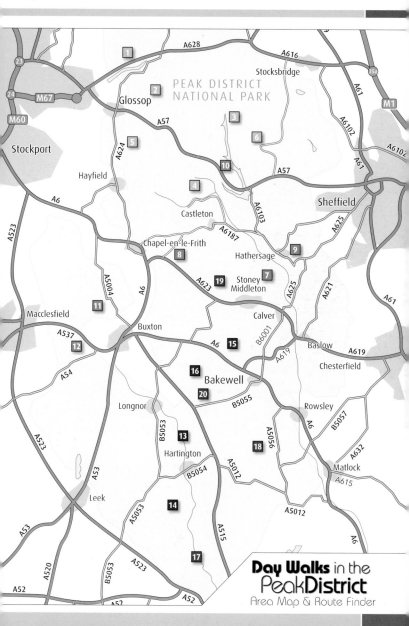

# SECTION 1

# The High Moors

*The walks in this category are located in the northern part of the Peak District. An area of bleak yet beckoning heather-clad moors, the habitat of red grouse, curlew and golden plover.*

*Remote gritstone crags stand guard over impressive, deeply cut valleys, down which tumble mountain streams, interjected with waterfalls and pools of peat-filtered water. This is also a land of man-made forests and reservoirs, that undeniably enhance the beauty of this upland landscape.*

KINDER DOWNFALL PHOTO: BARRY POPE

DERWENT DAM  PHOTO: JON BARTON

## 01 **Black Hill**

14km/8.7miles

Follows the Pennine Way up a craggy valley to a remote summit and descends by another well-trodden path along a broad ridge.

Crowden » Laddow Rocks » Black Hill » Towleyshaw Moor » Westend Moss » Crowden

## Start

**Crowden car park, just off the A628 Woodhead Pass road in the Longdendale Valley. GR: SK 073993.**

## The Walk

Crowden Campsite is normally the first night out for those who have embarked on the Pennine Way at Edale and completed the first tough section over Kinder Scout and Bleaklow. Our route tackles the next day's hike as far as the summit of Black Hill, before returning to Crowden via Tooleyshaw Moss and Hey Moss.

The Pennine Way takes us up the deep valley etched out by *Crowden Great Brook*, climbs more steeply to its western rim and then follows the narrow footpath that passes over the imposing gritstone crags of *Laddow Rocks*. Where the valley narrows to a gully, we follow the path beside the stream towards its source high on the moor. This necessitates fording several tributary streams and, except after a long, dry spell, gaiters are an indispensable item of clothing if we are to keep our feet dry!

Soon, the path becomes paved, and this continues for the last two kilometres to the summit of *Black Hill*, where the full Pennine panorama can be truly appreciated. The huge television mast at Holme Moss, two kilometres ESE of the summit cairn, dominates the eastern aspect but this seems not to detract from the wild, untamed ambience of the high moor.

From the summit, a compass bearing helps set us on the correct descent route, the initial few hundred metres requiring a creative approach to avoid bogs. Once past this, although there are other short, wet sections to negotiate, the path improves as it descends a broad ridge, passing *White Low* en route, offering views across the Longdendale Valley to the great bulk of Bleaklow.

---

**BLACK HILL**

**DISTANCE:** 14KM/8.7 MILES » **TOTAL ASCENT:** 488M/1,600 FT » **START GR:** SK 073993 » **TIME:** ALLOW 5 HOURS
**MAP:** OS EXPLORER OL1, THE DARK PEAK, 1:25,000 » **REFRESHMENTS:** NONE ON ROUTE » **NAVIGATION:** COMPETENCE IN THE USE OF MAP AND COMPASS IS STRONGLY ADVISED.

01 **BLACK HILL**

# **Directions** – Black Hill

**⑤➤** Walk to the toilet block and **turn right** up the walled lane. **Turn left** at the crossroads then **follow the track uphill** through a gate to a fingerpost on the right.

**2** **Take the Pennine Way path to Black Hill**. Follow this up the valley. After 2km the path climbs more steeply, crosses a stream, then continues up a paved section. Take the right fork along a narrow path running along the top of Laddow Rocks. Stay on this as it continues with a steep slope to the right. When the valley becomes a shallow gully, continue along the obvious path, **staying on the left side of the stream** (boggy in parts). Beyond the stream's source the path is paved for about 2km as it climbs to the cairn and trig' point at the summit of Black Hill.

**3** Black Hill (582m). From the cairn **walk south-east** (a magnetic bearing of 156° degrees in 2009), skirting the boggier areas. After 300m you will meet a fence with several stiles. Aim for the stile 30m right of a gate. Cross this and continue on the same bearing, aiming for a prominent cairn with a post. The path becomes more defined from this point and narrows down to a single thoroughfare. **Continue south** along the cairned footpath down a broad ridge, passing several ruined grouse butts. After descending to a saddle, continue uphill for a short distance to level ground on White Low.

**4** Follow the path, **now south-west,** pass right of a pool, then descend to a path junction.

> ▶OR▶ An alternative grass track can be taken right of the footpath after White Low. This takes a more westerly sweep but arrives at the same path junction.

**5** **Continue straight across** (or turn right if joining from the ▶OR▶) and follow the path downhill. This soon bears left and contours before descending once more to meet up with another grass track. **Bear left** and continue more or less on the level for 1km to where the track bends left beneath spoil heaps.

**6** **Fork right** down to a stile. Descend steeply. After crossing two further stiles **turn left** on a track and return to the car park.

# 02 **Bleaklow Head**

20.6km/12.8 miles

A demanding 'mountain' walk to a remote summit using the Pennine Way in ascent and a Roman Road in descent.

Old Glossop » Padfield » Torside Reservoir » Bleaklow Head » Doctor's Gate » Old Glossop

## Start

Turn off the A57 to Old Glossop along Church Street, then bear right up Shepley Street to park alongside the factory. GR: SK 043947.

## The Walk

This route climbs out of Old Glossop by a combination of track and footpath. To avoid walking along tarmac, it wends a way across fields, through a cemetery, and past cottages, eventually descending to the *Trans Pennine Trail*. The walking here is easy but would become monotonous if it were not for the changing views of the reservoirs and the steep flanking moors.

On leaving the Trail, the climb along the *Pennine Way* up Bleaklow begins in earnest, the first half kilometre being steep, although not difficult underfoot. It gradually eases off and takes on the character of a mountain path, enhanced by its course along the rim of the steep-sided and craggy *Torside Clough*.

After nearly five kilometres of climbing, the summit cairn at *Bleaklow Head* reveals itself. 'Bleak' is an apt description of this barren, eroded summit mound. In bad weather one can quickly become disoriented here, and even in clear conditions, when there are distant views of the Pennines to the north and the Lancashire and Cheshire plains to the west, the routes off the summit are not clearly defined, and a compass becomes an essential navigational aid.

Once located, the Pennine Way footpath becomes a well-blazed trail that is followed towards the summit of the *Snake Pass*. Before reaching the pass, however, the Pennine Way crosses a much older pathway known as *Doctor's Gate*; an old Roman Road. This is our means of descent, a mountain path that is anything but a 'road' as it descends an impressive valley back to to Old Glossop.

---

### BLEAKLOW HEAD

DISTANCE: 20.6KM/12.8 MILES » **TOTAL ASCENT:** 651M/2,135 FT » **START GR:** SK 043947 » **TIME:** ALLOW 6 HOURS **MAP:** OS EXPLORER OL1 THE DARK PEAK 1:25,000 » **REFRESHMENTS:** NONE ON ROUTE » **NAVIGATION:** COMPETENCE IN THE USE OF MAP AND COMPASS IS STRONGLY ADVISED.

02 **BLEAKLOW HEAD**

# Directions – Bleaklow Head

**⊙►** Walk up Church Street South and pass immediately right of the Bulls Head Public House. **Turn right** on Bute Street and continue to Shire Hill Hospital entrance. **Turn right** to follow the tarmac lane around the right-hand perimeter of the hospital.

**2** 100m after passing a pond, and opposite farm buildings, **turn left to cross a footbridge** and follow a path up the side of an embankment. Continue with the reservoir wall on your right. Keep **straight ahead** across two stiles and continue uphill to a road.

**3** **Turn right** at the road, and **then left** on a path beside a cottage. This leads to a stile straight ahead, not easily seen. **Continue straight ahead, then bear half right** to a stile in the cemetery wall. Cross this, **bear right to the chapel**, and continue along a drive alongside the right-hand boundary wall. Your objective is a stile in this wall between rhododendrons about 100m before the drive joins the road ahead.

**4** **Cross the stile** and **bear half right** towards a wall corner. **Descend to the left** to join an old track running alongside a pond. Leave the track to keep straight on along a footpath that meets the road in the village of Padfield.

**5** **Turn left** and after 100m **turn right** between cottages (fingerpost). Continue down the track. **Cross the first stile on the left** and descend to the TransPennine Trail. **Turn right** along this and follow it for 3km, at which point it crosses a road.

**6** **Turn right**, cross the road and **turn left** up a track to join the Pennine Way. This soon leaves the track and ascends steeply for about 800m before becoming more gradual. **Fork left** down to the stream to cross Torside Clough at a ford. *(Another path keeps straight on but becomes indistinct as it approaches the summit.)* Continue along the Pennine Way to the cairn at Bleaklow Head.

**7** Bleaklow Head (633m). **Care is needed on leaving the summit**. By walking SSW from the cairn (a magnetic bearing of around 217° in 2009) you will pick up the Pennine Way footpath. This becomes an obvious and waymarked route using stream channels, and short sections are paved. The path crosses two fords and after 3km a crossroads of paths is reached with a post identifying the spot. The path cutting across the Pennine Way is Doctor's Gate.

**8** **Turn right** to follow Doctor's Gate down the valley. This crosses a boggy area and a footbridge en route. After 3km it joins a former quarry track. Follow this downhill to Old Glossop. **Keep straight ahead** alongside factory premises to return to the start.

FOOTBRIDGE ACROSS SHELF BROOK, DOCTOR'S GATE  PHOTO: NORMAN TAYLOR

WILFREY NEILD, WILFREY EDGE  PHOTO: MAUREEN POPE

# 03 Margery Hill & Howden Edge    14km/8.75 miles

An excursion to the highest point in South Yorkshire that has many of the characteristics of a Lakeland fell walk.

Kings Tree » Slippery Stones » Margery Hill » Howden Edge » Howden Reservoir »
Slippery Stones » Kings Tree

## Start

Kings Tree in the Upper Derwent Valley. (GR: SK 168938.) Parking is not permitted at weekends and on Bank Holidays, when bus transport from Fairholmes car park is available.

## The Walk

From the turning circle at Kings Tree a forest track leads us out into open country, to a crossing point of the youthful River Derwent known as *Slippery Stones*. Upstream of, and visible from the bridge, this is where the river was originally forded. The ancient packhorse bridge now used for the crossing was originally located further down the valley but was dismantled and re-erected in its present position when the Ladybower Dam was constructed in the first half of the 20th century.

The gentle walking up to this point soon gives way to hill climbing as we begin the ascent onto the moors. Steep at first, the slope soon relents and the climb becomes more gradual as we cross open moor en route to the broad escarpment and summit of *Margery Hill*.

The views are extensive; distant landmarks to the east and north identify the industry of South and West Yorkshire, whilst the high moors and broad, rounded ridges of Bleaklow and Kinder Scout dominate the western horizon.

A footpath along the rim of *Howden Edge* leads us south, high alongside the plateau of Featherbed Moss, after which a descent is made to the banks of *Howden Reservoir*. Our initial gentle pace is rediscovered, as we follow a lakeside track around the eastern flank of the reservoir, to return via *Slippery Stones* to *Kings Tree*.

---

## MARGERY HILL & HOWDEN EDGE

**DISTANCE:** 14KM/8.75 MILES » **TOTAL ASCENT:** 516M/1,692FT » **START GR:** SK 168938 » **TIME:** ALLOW 5–5.5 HOURS
**MAP:** OS EXPLORER OL1, THE DARK PEAK, 1:25,000 » **REFRESHMENTS:** NONE ON ROUTE **NAVIGATION:** ALTHOUGH THE WHOLE ROUTE IS ON CLEAR PATHS, PROFICIENCY IN MAP AND COMPASS USE IS ADVISED.

*MOUNTAIN HARE PHOTO: BARRY POPE*

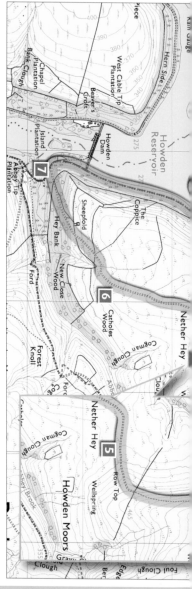

## 03 MARGERY HILL & HOWDEN EDGE

➲ Go through the gate and follow the forest track across a ford and gradually uphill. This leads to the old packhorse bridge at Slippery Stones. **Cross it and bear left**, cross a footbridge and **fork right** (bridleway to Langsett).

**2** Follow the path up the narrow valley, cross the stream and continue steeply, taking either of two paths – the easier-angled one being the bridleway. The paths join before veering left above old quarries. Continue ascending on easier-angled terrain for some distance. Pass two cairns and continue to a third cairn and a footpath crossroads on level ground.

**3** **Turn right** and take the often-boggy path that runs south-east to the trig' point at the summit of Margery Hill, keeping left of an enclosure protecting an ancient site.

**4** Margery Hill (546m). From the nearby Margery Stones **bear half right** (SSW) along a footpath that becomes vague just before it joins the narrow path that runs along the top of Wilfrey Edge. **Turn left** and follow the edge footpath up to the cairn at High Stones. **Keep straight ahead**, staying on the right of, and parallel with, a man-made dyke on the left. The path descends gradually for just over a kilometre and then passes through the remains of a wall. Immediately after the wall the path/track bends right and zigzags down a steep slope to arrive at a saddle (level ground), and a fork in the track.

**5** **Fork right**. After a further 100m follow the path as it bears left uphill. After levelling out, this descends to join a well-used track.

**6** **Turn right** and follow this track to and through a gate. Continue descending to join the track that runs above and alongside Howden Reservoir.

**7** **Turn right**. Continue for 3km along the track beside the reservoir to the bridge at Slippery Stones. Cross the bridge and retrace your steps to Kings Tree.

# 04 **Kinder Scout – South-east Circuit**  15.8km/9.8 miles

The easiest ascent of Kinder Scout and fine traverse of its impressive, steep, southern flanks and craggy tors.

Edale » Ollerbrook Booth » Jaggers Clough » Crookstone Knoll » Ringing Roger »
Grindslow Knoll » Edale

## Start

**Edale Pay and Display car park. GR: SK 124853.**

## The Walk

Leaving *Edale* we soon reach the tiny hamlet at *Ollerbrook Booth*, one of several 'booths' in the Vale of Edale. The term has ancient origins and was used to denote a livestock enclosure.

Continuing north-east, we flank Kinder's south-eastern slopes, meeting up with the bridleway that links the Vale of Edale with the Derwent woodlands and valleys.

The packhorse drivers were known as 'Jaggers' – a little further on the bridleway crosses *Jaggers Clough* at a ford. The steep climb from the ford gives an idea of what these laden packhorses were capable of.

After levelling out, the bridleway reaches a junction with the Roman Road, an even more ancient roadway. We follow this for a short distance before breaking off on a footpath that makes a gradual ascent across open moor to *Crookstone Knoll*, on the edge of the Kinder plateau. A splendid viewpoint from which to take in the majestic surroundings.

The path undulates gently as it traverses above the steep flanks of Kinder from east to west, crossing gullies that form deeply incised valleys below. On reaching the promontory of rocks at *Ringing Roger*, our route clings to the top of the crags that hover impressively over Grindsbrook Clough, before we head south to the high point on *Grindslow Knoll*.

Our descent from here is gradual and soon we re-enter *Edale* opposite the Nag's Head, a fitting place to celebrate a fine day's walk.

---

## KINDER SCOUT – SOUTH–EAST CIRCUIT

**DISTANCE:** 15.8KM/9.8MILES » **TOTAL ASCENT:** 662M/2,170FT » **START GR:** SK 124853 » **TIME:** ALLOW 5.5 – 6 HOURS
**MAP:** OS EXPLORER OL 1, THE DARK PEAK, 1:25,000 » **REFRESHMENTS:** NAG'S HEAD, THE RAMBLERS AND CAFÉ AT EDALE
**NAVIGATION:** ALTHOUGH THE WHOLE ROUTE IS ON CLEAR PATHS, PROFICIENCY IN MAP AND COMPASS USE IS ADVISED.

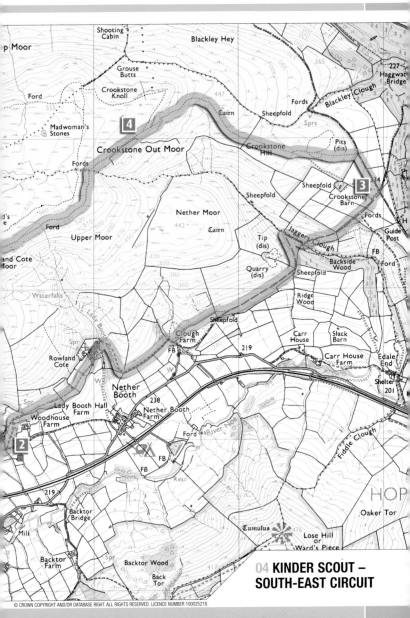

04 KINDER SCOUT – SOUTH-EAST CIRCUIT

# **Directions** – Kinder Scout – South-east Circuit

**➌** Leave the car park and **turn right** up the road to Edale. Immediately beyond the Visitor Centre **take the path on the right**. Keep **straight ahead** and through the small hamlet of Ollerbrook Booth. Stay on the same course along a track. Where this bends left up to a cottage, continue straight ahead for a further 300m and look for the path going left up a field.

**2** Follow this path uphill then bear right above a wood. Continue to Edale Youth Hostel. Pass directly in front of the main building and descend to cross a footbridge. The narrow path bears right initially. Stay on this. It soon descends to cross a gully and then climbs steeply before joining a track. Continue uphill along the track, then drop down into Jaggers Clough, across a ford and climb steeply uphill to reach a crossroads of tracks.

**3** **Turn left** and follow the track (Roman Road) for 400m and go through a gate. **Turn left** off the track onto the footpath. Continue past trees. The path climbs gradually to and past a gritstone crag. Stay on the most obvious path heading south-west. This joins the path that runs around the edge of the plateau.

**4** Continue south-west. The undulating path crosses a gully, after which **take the higher of the two paths** leading on from the gully *(NOT the higher level path shown on the OS map, which runs parallel 100 metres up to the right)*. Continue across the top of the steep gully of Lady Booth Brook to the top of the next major gully at Ollerbrook Clough. 100m beyond this look for a stile in the fence on the right.

**5** **Either** cross this and head northwest to cross another stile and follow the path to the top of the next clough (Golden Clough), **or** stay on the edge footpath and follow this across the top of the Ringing Roger promontory to reach the same point.

**6** Continue along the edge footpath. After 2km the path is forced north above a deeply incised gully to a point where the stream can be crossed safely. It then heads south to the head of Grindsbrook Clough. Continue along the edge then climb to the summit of Grindslow Knoll.

**7** Grindslow Knoll (601m). For a pleasant descent from the cairn, head south down and off the ridge. On meeting another path **bear left**, then **left again almost immediately**. After 200m **bear left** again to walk alongside a wall and descend to join the main path descending more directly from Grindslow Knoll. **Turn right**. Follow the path downhill to the road at Edale. **Turn right** to return to the car park.

*THE ANVIL ABOVE GRINDSBROOK  PHOTO: BARRY POPE*

## 05 **Kinder Downfall from Hayfield**     14.8km/9.2miles

A classic mountain walk around the craggy amphitheatre home to Kinder Scout's most spectacular feature, the Downfall.

Hayfield » White Brow » William Clough » Ashop Head » Kinder Downfall » Kinder Low » Kinderlow End » Bowden Bridge » Hayfield

## Start

Sett Valley Trail car park, Hayfield. GR: SK 036869.

## The Walk

From the village of *Hayfield* we follow an ancient pathway up on to the lower flanks of Kinder Scout. After the initial climb the path levels out along *White Brow*, high above Kinder Reservoir with a breathtaking view of the craggy amphitheatre guarding Kinder's western approach.

The climb begins again up the narrow confines of *William Clough*, where the mountain path crosses and re-crosses the stream as it snakes uphill for a kilometre to join the Pennine Way on the col at *Ashop Head*. Another steep climb on a paved path leads to easier ground on the edge of the summit plateau.

With much ascent behind us, we follow a gently undulating footpath to the spectacular craggy landscape of *Kinder Downfall*. The River Kinder often struggles to be a 'waterfall' over the sandstone cliffs as the prevailing westerly winds blow the water back up in an impressive spray display.

After drinking in the dramatic scenery, we continue along the Pennine Way as it follows the edge of the plateau, the view westward stretching beyond the Cheshire plain to the Welsh hills. Soon we arrive at *Kinder Low*. At 633m above sea level, with a trig' pillar and huge cairn, this eroded spot is as near to a summit as Kinder possesses, although the highest point is in fact 3m higher and 800m northwest.

Our descent follows a path down a delightful ridge, past *Kinderlow End* and then through farmland and picks up a riverside path at *Bowden Bridge*, which is followed back into Hayfield.

---

### KINDER DOWNFALL FROM HAYFIELD

**DISTANCE:** 14.8KM/9.2MILES » **TOTAL ASCENT:** 610M/2,000FT » **START GR:** SK 036869 » **TIME:** ALLOW 5.5 HOURS
**MAP:** OS EXPLORER OL1, THE DARK PEAK, 1:25,000 » **REFRESHMENTS:** NONE ON ROUTE » **NAVIGATION:** COMPETENCE IN THE USE OF MAP AND COMPASS IS STRONGLY ADVISED.

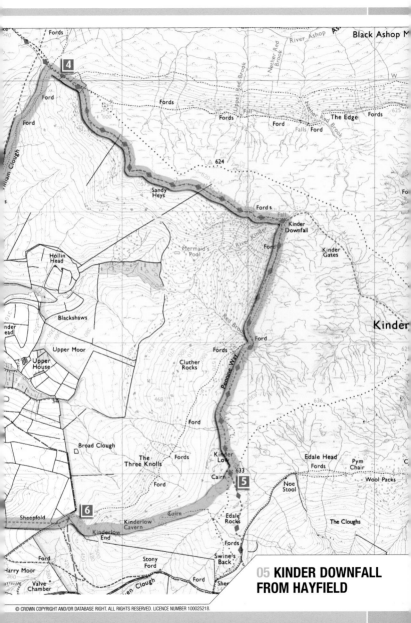

**05 KINDER DOWNFALL FROM HAYFIELD**

# **Directions** – Kinder Downfall from Hayfield

**➊** From the car park **cross the main road** that divides Hayfield and walk beside the church to the road in the village. **Turn left**, cross the bridge then keep **straight ahead** up Bank Street. **Bear right** along Kinder Road to a bridleway sign on the left after 400m.

**2** **Turn left**. Follow the bridleway (Snake Path) uphill. When the path levels out, pass through a gate and **bear right** along the Snake Path. Continue for another 500m to a path junction on the approach to a shooting cabin.

**3** **Turn right** and then **bear left** after 70m at the *Public Bridleway* sign. Follow the narrow path around the hillside above the reservoir. A very gradual descent leads to William Clough. The path now climbs beside the stream for just over a kilometre, where paving stones are followed to a junction with the Pennine Way at Ashop Head.

**➌** Paving stones cut the corner here, joining the Pennine Way south-east of point **4**.

**4** **Bear right** and climb steeply up the paved path that leads up to the summit plateau. Follow the path south-east to Kinder Downfall. Cross the River Kinder and continue along the summit rim, now in a south–westerly direction. After a kilometre the path fords a stream (Red Brook). Stay on the more used footpath. This climbs in stages over the next kilometre to the huge cairn on Kinder Low, smaller cairns helping to keep you on course for the last few hundred metres.

**5** **Kinder Low** (633m). From the cairn walk on a magnetic bearing of around 203 degrees in 2009 (approx SSW) to a smaller but still prominent cairn about 150m away. Still following the same bearing, after a few metres the footpath becomes paved. Follow this. Further on, the paved path forks. **Keep straight ahead (right fork)**. This leads to the fenced-off Bronze Age bowl barrow. Continue past this and on down the ridge, finally descending steeply via a well-constructed stone staircase. Continue to a stile by a gate on the left at the base of the steep slope.

**6** Cross this and fork right to another stile and gate. Cross this and descend fields via stiles and gateways to Tunstead Clough Farm. Follow the concrete track past the cottages and downhill to a junction with a road. **Turn right** and follow this to Bowden Bridge.

**7** **Do not cross the bridge** but keep straight ahead towards the campsite reception building. Pass right of this and follow the riverside path. The path eventually joins a track, which becomes Valley Road. Follow this back into the village. **Turn right**, descend the main street and **turn left** by the church to reach the car park.

*KINDER RESERVOIR FROM THE DOWNFALL  PHOTO: BARRY POPE*

BOOT'S FOLLY FROM BROGGING END  PHOTO: JOHN COEFIELD

# 06 **Derwent Edge from Bradfield**    20.5km/12.7miles

A lengthy but varied outing with outstanding views featuring woodland, lakeside, moorland and high craggy tors.

Low Bradfield » Blindside Lane » Sugworth Edge » Moscar » Derwent Edge » Back Tor » Strines Bridge » Brogging » Dale Road » Low Bradfield

## Start

Low Bradfield. Car park next to the village playground, off Fairhouse Lane uphill from the bridge. GR: SK 262920.

## The Walk

From the village of *Low Bradfield* we begin our route along a riverside path. A short stretch up the quiet *Blindside Lane* gives access to a forest path above Dale Dike Reservoir. Beyond this the route crosses open fields from which one can appreciate the 'lakeland' setting hereabouts. On approaching Strines Dam we climb the flanking hillside before reaching level ground below *Sugworth Edge*, then pass Boot's Folly, a prominent tower that local magnate Charles Boot built in 1926-27 to provide employment for his stonemasons.

A short section of road follows that links up with the paths that lead onto the heather moors of *Derwent Edge*. We pass numerous shooting butts, this being the habitat of the red grouse. On arriving at the crest of the escarpment an outstanding view of Ladybower Reservoir and the surrounding hills is revealed.

Our route follows *Derwent Edge* past the prominent craggy tors and rocks eroded into fabulous shapes, notably the Coach and Horses (shown as the Wheel Stones on the OS map), the Salt Cellar and the Cakes of Bread. After 3km, the highest point of the walk is reached: *Back Tor* (538m), where one can savour the panorama before descending.

The way down is more abrupt than the route taken in ascent. With much height lost, take a short diversion from *Strines Bridge* to pay a visit to 15th century Strines Inn. Back on route, our descent continues past Strines Reservoir and down to the banks of Dale Dike Reservoir, where a very pleasant path is followed through woodland alongside the reservoir. The dam here was built to replace the one that collapsed in 1864 causing Sheffield's Great Flood. From here, the quiet lane of Dale Road leads back into *Low Bradfield*.

---

### DERWENT EDGE FROM BRADFIELD

**DISTANCE:** 20.5KM/12.7MILES » **TOTAL ASCENT:** 605M/1,982FT » **START GR:** SK 262920 » **TIME:** ALLOW 6 HOURS
**MAP:** OS EXPLORER OL1, THE DARK PEAK, 1:25,000 » **REFRESHMENTS:** STRINES INN JUST OFF ROUTE ON THE DESCENT. THE PLOUGH AND TEA SHOP AT LOW BRADFIELD; OLD HORNS AT HIGH BRADFIELD » **NAVIGATION:** STRAIGHTFORWARD.

**06 DERWENT EDGE
FROM BRADFIELD**

# **Directions** – Derwent Edge from Bradfield

**➍** Walk back to the road, **turn left** and keep straight on as far as The Plough public house. **Take the track on the right** just beyond the pub. Follow this and its footpath continuation to a lane (Blindside Lane).

**2** **Turn left** and follow the lane uphill, passing two cottages. After approx. 1km **cross a stile on the right** next to a gate. Continue along the forest track and then along a path across fields via stiles. Cross a footbridge of railway sleepers and cross a stile on the right of a gate.

**3** Keep straight ahead along the gradually ascending footpath and through gateposts without a gate. Follow the path uphill above Strines Reservoir. The path passes left of Boot's Folly and heads for the boundary wall of Sugworth Hall. Pass through the gate, cross a stile and continue through the rhododendron tunnel to emerge at the drive. Continue uphill to exit the property by a gate and stile.

**4** **Turn right** and follow the road for 1km to a T-junction. **Go straight across** and through the gate opposite. Follow the path down to, and past, Moscar House via two gates. **Keep straight ahead along the track only as far as a gate**.

**5** **Turn right** and follow the path uphill with a wall on the left. Pass through a gate at the top of the rise and follow the track/path across a stream and then uphill alongside grouse butts. A path crossroads is reached on Derwent Edge.

**6** **Turn right**. Follow the gradually ascending path along Derwent Edge for 3km to the trig' point at Back Tor.

**7** Back Tor (538m). After a breather at the Tor, retrace your steps along the paving stones to a path crossroads marked by a prominent upstanding boundary stone (Bradfield Gate). **Turn left** and follow the path downhill. This joins a tarmac lane at a cattle grid. Continue descending to emerge at a road. *(The Strines Inn is 300 metres uphill to the right.)*

**8**  **Turn left**. Follow the road uphill for 600m to a track on the right for Stubbing Farm. **Turn right**. Follow the track downhill as far as the first cottage.

**9**  **Turn right**, then **bear left** down to a stile. The path descends beneath Strines Dam. Cross a footbridge and **bear left** on the Permissive Path and cross another footbridge. Follow the path alongside Dale Dike Reservoir. Exit by the dam and keep straight ahead as waymarked. Follow a track to a road.

**10**  **Turn right** and follow the road downhill. Either stay on this back to Bradfield (1.5km), or take the first road on the right after 800m, cross Annet Bridge, turn left at the stile and retrace your steps back to the village.

*THE SALT CELLAR  PHOTO: BARRY POPE*

# SECTION 2

# Hills, Tors & Edges

*The area in which the walks in this category fall is located to the south of the high moors and includes the eastern and western borderlands of the Peak District. Here the landscape is characterised by broad ridges, hilltops, and gritstone tors and edges, particularly those famous 'eastern edges' – such as Stanage, Burbage, Froggatt and Curbar – that stand tall, looking west across the Peak.*

*A varied landscape, with wooded river valleys and cloughs, wild meadows, pasture and farmland; of lower lying moor dotted with stone circles and other ancient relics.*

THE 'APPARENT NORTH' BUTTRESS AT THE SOUTHERN END OF STANAGE EDGE (WALK 9) PHOTO: JOHN COEFIELD

WINTER SUNRISE ACROSS MAM TOR AND THE HOPE VALLEY (WALK 8)  PHOTO: JOHN COEFIELD

SIR WILLIAM HILL SUMMIT TRIG POINT  PHOTO: JOHN COEFIELD

# 07 Sir William Hill from Eyam

16.4km/10.2miles

A varied walk from the plague village of Eyam, taking in riverside, a secluded wooded valley and a climb to open moor.

Eyam » Stoney Middleton » Froggatt » Grindleford Bridge » Leadmill Bridge » Stoke Ford » Sir William Hill » Eyam

## Start

Eyam, Pay and Display car park on the west side of the village. GR: SK 216767.

## The Walk

*Eyam* is one of the White Peak's larger villages. It is probably best known for its connection with the bubonic plague in the 17th century. Indeed our walk passes the village victims' cottages and the churchyard where many of them were buried.

Leaving *Eyam* we take the path that passes the Boundary Stone, where villagers left money in the coin slots in exchange for food and other goods brought up from *Stoney Middleton*. Our route descends from here and passes through the older part of Stoney with its narrow streets and quaint old cottages.

Striking out across fields from Stoney, we descend to the banks of the River Derwent where a path is followed upstream and crosses the river at *Froggatt* by the beautiful stone bridge whose width declares its antiquity. Beyond *Froggatt* we leave the riverside and pass through stretches of indigenous woodland alternating with riverside pasture, before crossing the river at *Leadmill Bridge*.

Our route takes the path up the secluded valley formed by Highlow Brook. This rises and falls as it passes in and out of woodland and across gullies to reach an ideal picnic spot at *Stoke Ford*. From here a stiff climb winds up to a viewpoint on *Sir William Hill*. The views on the way up and from the top are sufficient reward for our effort.

A short level section with views across the White Peak is soon followed by a sharp descent back down to *Eyam*.

---

## SIR WILLIAM HILL FROM EYAM

**DISTANCE:** 16.4KM/10.2MILES » **TOTAL ASCENT:** 477M/1,565FT » **START GR:** SK 216767 » **TIME:** ALLOW 5–5.5 HOURS **MAP:** OS EXPLORER OL1 (THE DARK PEAK) AND OL24 (THE WHITE PEAK), BOTH 1:25,000 » **REFRESHMENTS:** THE PLOUGH INN AT LEADMILL BRIDGE; A CHOICE OF TEASHOPS AND MINER'S ARMS IN EYAM » **NAVIGATION:** STRAIGHTFORWARD.

**07 SIR WILLIAM HILL FROM EYAM**

# Directions – Sir William Hill from Eyam

**⑤➤** Walk down the road to the junction, **turn left** and continue through the village, past the church to the junction at the village centre. **Bear left** and **turn right** up Lydgate. Where the lane bears left downhill, **keep straight ahead** as for the Boundary Stone. Follow the path to the Stone and continue downhill to Stoney Middleton.

**②** **Turn right** on the lane and continue along the village back street. Where this bends right to cross a bridge, **take the road to the left**. Follow this around the left side of the church to a left-hand bend. **Keep straight ahead** here through a gate. After a second gate **take the path that forks left**. This climbs the hillside then passes through Knouchley Farm via two gates. Continue down the drive to the main road. Cross this and go through the gate opposite. Head straight down to the bottom of the field, **bear left** through a gap and descend to join the riverside footpath.

**③** **Turn left**, follow the path to the bridge at Froggatt, cross it and **turn left** into Hollowgate. **Keep straight ahead** where the road bends right, and follow the path to Grindleford Bridge. Cross the road, **turn right and take the path on the left** in 100m (Derwent Valley Heritage Trail). Follow this along riverside pastures for 3.5km to emerge at the road at Leadmill Bridge.

**④** **Turn left**, cross the bridge and **take the second road on the right**. Follow this, or the path running parallel on the left of the hedge, uphill to a hairpin bend. **Keep straight ahead** here along a track. Pass through two gates. **Keep straight ahead**, ignoring other options. The path passes through a wood where it can be muddy and awkward underfoot in wet conditions, then descends to ford a stream. A climb follows, then another descent to cross a second stream, and yet another short climb and descent to reach Stoke Ford.

**⑤** Instead of crossing the footbridge, **bear left and fork left almost immediately** to follow the winding path up the steep hillside. The path levels out. Cross a stile leading to access land.

**⑥** **Take the middle path of three**. This leads directly up onto the moor. Follow this to the top of the hillside and keep straight ahead to arrive at a track (Sir William Hill Road). Cross this and the stile opposite. Follow the path to join a road after a stile.

**7** **Turn right**. Follow the road to Highcliffe Farm, **turn left** and follow the track steeply downhill to return to Eyam.

PLAGUE COTTAGE

Mary Hadfield, formerly Cooper, lived here with her two sons, Edward and Jonathan, her new husband, Alexander Hadfield and an employed hand George Viccars

George Viccars, the first plague victim, died on 7th September 1665
Edward Cooper, aged 4 died on the 22nd September 1665
Jonathan Cooper, aged 12, died on the 2nd October 1665
Alexander Hadfield died on the 3rd August 1666
Mary alone survived but lost 13 relatives

*PLAGUE COTTAGE, EYAM  PHOTO: JOHN COEFIELD*

# 08 Lord's Seat & Eldon Hill

16.7km/10.4miles

Traverse a high moorland ridge overlooking Edale and pass over the contrasting terrain of the limestone hill country west of Castleton.

Castleton » Mam Nick » Lord's Seat » Perry Dale » Old Dam » Eldon Hill » Hurd Low » Castleton

## Start

Castleton, Pay and Display car park. GR: SK 149829.

## The Walk

*Castleton* and its show caverns draw in huge numbers of tourists year round. As its name implies, the village owes its origins to the 11th century castle, whose construction began soon after the Norman Conquest by William Peveril, an illegitimate son of William the Conqueror.

Climbing out of *Castleton* our route passes The Devil's Arse, Treak Cliff and Blue John Caverns; the latter is named after the 'bleu-jaune' or blue-yellow mineral mined here, whilst the first is the nom de plume of Peak Cavern, the entrance to which is a huge, gaping hole!

Leaving the caverns, we make for *Mam Nick*, the gap in the Great Ridge separating Mam Tor from Rushup Edge. The underlying rock here is in layers of sandstone and shale. The shale is soft and easily eroded, resulting in the spectacular landslip features on Mam Tor's eastern face and along the northern flanks of Rushup Edge, clearly seen as we progress up the ridge.

After reaching the high point of Rushup Edge at *Lord's Seat*, the next 6km is in descent, first along the ridge and then along quiet lanes in limestone country, all in preparation for the next climb amongst rocky outcrops up the flanks of *Eldon Hill*.

We connect with tracks and field paths that lead across high pasture west of Castleton. Reaching a point near the back of the keep at Peveril Castle, there is a good view into Cave Dale. As with nearby Winnats Pass, it is believed that Cave Dale was etched out of the landscape by glacier meltwater torrent as the ice receded.

A gradually descending path wends its way down to *Castleton*, and provides fine views of the village and the Great Ridge from Mam Tor to Lose Hill.

## LORD'S SEAT & ELDON HILL

**DISTANCE:** 16.7KM/10.4MILES » **TOTAL ASCENT:** 565M/1,854FT » **START GR:** SK 149829 » **TIME:** ALLOW 5.5–6 HOURS **MAP:** OS EXPLORER OL1 (THE DARK PEAK) AND OL24 (THE WHITE PEAK), BOTH 1:25,000 » **REFRESHMENTS:** PUBS AND CAFÉS IN CASTLETON » **NAVIGATION:** STRAIGHTFORWARD.

# 08 LORD'S SEAT & ELDON HILL

# **Directions** – Lord's Seat & Eldon Hill

**➎** Cross the main road from the car park entrance and walk past the front of Three Roofs Café. Continue on the pedestrian path alongside the river to a junction. **Turn right** and follow the road uphill, go through a gate and follow the path to Speedwell Cavern. **Cross the road** and follow the path for Treak Cliff Cavern. **Do not descend to the car park – keep straight ahead**. Pass through the break in the railings to join the main path ascending to the cavern. Pass above the premises, waymarked, and continue uphill to Blue John Cavern. **Turn right** and continue up to the old road.

**2** **Turn left**. Continue up the road for 300m, **cross a stile on the right** and follow the path uphill to the road at Mam Nick.

**3** **Turn left**, cross the road and pass through a gate. Continue uphill on the bridleway and **bear right** after 200m up onto the ridge footpath. Follow the path for 1.3km to the high point at Lord's Seat. Continue along Rushup Edge for a further 2km, now in descent. Where the path meets the road, take the concession footpath alongside the wall running right to a gate in 150m.

**4** **Cross the main road** and follow the road opposite downhill. On reaching a road junction **turn left** and then **take the road on the right**. Follow this for approx 2km to the point where Eldon Lane joins from the left at a speed limit sign.

**5** **Turn left here** and continue up the lane and its continuation track. After passing through a gate, continue uphill along the bridleway. This keeps close to the wall on the right. Stay on this course, keeping close to the wall. The bridleway eventually emerges at a track.

**6** **Turn right** and follow the track. This joins another track after the second gate. **Continue straight ahead** to another gate.

**7** **Pass through this and turn left** to pass through another gate immediately. Follow the waymarked path (Limestone Way) across a field and down into a small valley. Leave the bridleway here and **keep straight ahead (left)** along the waymarked footpath up a narrow strip of field. Continue across a stile then **bear slightly right** to follow the obvious field path downhill. This heads for trees in the distance. About 100m before reaching the trees (and the castle keep hidden behind them), the path doubles back downhill to the left. Descend to a footpath junction and turn right to retrace the outward route back into Castleton.

GATE LATCH ON RUSHUP EDGE BRIDLEWAY **PHOTO:** BARRY POPE

# 09 **Hathersage Moor** 17.2km/10.7miles

Riverside paths, a wooded gorge, an Iron Age fort, a prominent tor and a gritstone edge.

Hathersage » Padley » Toad's Mouth » Carl Wark » Higger Tor » Burbage Bridge » Stanage Edge »
Long Causeway » Hathersage

## Start

**Hathersage, Pay and Display car park.
GR: SK 231814.**

## The Walk

Setting off from the Dark Peak hub of
*Hathersage*, we walk with the River
Derwent and up through delightful,
unspoilt woodland to *Padley*. The chapel,
now a museum, is all that remains of 15th
century Padley Hall.

Our path leads up beside Burbage Brook
through ancient oak and birch woodland
and crosses Padley Gorge, where it certainly
takes on the character of a true gorge.
We emerge from the woodland into wild
pasture; the brook and surrounding moor a
popular picnic spot in the summer months.

After crossing the road at *Toad's Mouth*,
our route ascends moorland to the rocky
tor of Carl Wark, the stone walls here the
remains of an Iron Age fort. We climb
again to the summit of *Higger Tor* (434m),
a fine point to take in the 360 degree
view. The south-facing 'leaning block' of

*Higger Tor* is a distinctive local landmark,
often draped in rock climbers and full of
climbing history.

From *Higger Tor*, the walk heads for
*Burbage Bridge* before gently climbing to
the top of *Stanage Edge*, a 5km long
gritstone edge and world famous rock
climbing crag. Stanage is the king of the
Eastern Edges; a spine of gritstone crags
that stretch from the Derwent Moors in
the north to Chatsworth Park and beyond
in the south.

All too soon we descend along the ancient
track known as the *Long Causeway*. This
links with footpaths that descend gently in
stages to *Hathersage*.

## HATHERSAGE MOOR

**DISTANCE:** 17.2KM/10.7MILES » **TOTAL ASCENT:** 448M/1,470FT » **START GR:** SK 231814 » **TIME:** ALLOW 5.5 HOURS
**MAP:** OS EXPLORER OL1, THE DARK PEAK, 1:25,000 » **REFRESHMENTS:** GRINDLEFORD STATION CAFÉ AT PADLEY. MOBILE
REFRESHMENTS AT BURBAGE BRIDGE » **NAVIGATION:** STRAIGHTFORWARD.

**09 HATHERSAGE MOOR**

# **Directions** – Hathersage Moor

**❻** **Turn right** out of the car park and walk to the road junction. Cross the road, **turn left** and then **take the first road on the right**. Follow this under the railway bridge and down to the right-hand bend. **Turn left** on the path here. Follow this through meadows to emerge at Leadmill Bridge. Cross the road and continue alongside the river. As the path approaches cottages the footpath diverts to the right through a gate. Continue across riverside pastures for about 1km, then enter woodland.

**2** About 150m into the woodland (Coppice Wood) **bear left uphill** away from the riverside path. The path exits the wood at a gate. **Bear slightly right** on a field path. This soon runs along the left side of a wall to a wood facing with open gateway on the right.

**3** **Turn left** here then **keep straight ahead** along the field edge, pass over a railway bridge and join a track. **Turn right**, pass Padley Chapel and a row of terraced houses, and descend to pass more cottages and the old mill. The unmade road crosses Burbage Brook.

**4** **Turn left** immediately after passing over the bridge and follow the easiest and most obvious footpath up through woods with the brook on your left. After 400m or so, descend steps to the left to **cross the gorge** by a footbridge. **Continue uphill** to join a major footpath. **Turn right** and follow the path above and parallel with the brook through woods, then open ground. Pass a footbridge and continue to a second.

**5** **Bear left** up to the main road. Cross this and the stile opposite, and then **fork right** to climb above Toad's Mouth rock. Continue to the rocky tor and Iron Age fort of Carl Wark, entering it by the south-west gateway. **Keep straight ahead**, descend from the north-west gateway and follow the path uphill to Higger Tor. The main path becomes a scramble amongst rocks but an easier option is available by bearing left to a gap in the crags. Return to the eastern edge then resume the former direction. **Keep straight ahead**, ignoring a left fork further on, descend from the tor, then continue straight on – road to your left – to Burbage Bridge.

**6** **Cross the stile** on the left into the car park, walk to the road and **turn left**. Continue to the left-hand bend but **keep straight ahead** here along the path heading for the crags of Stanage Edge. Follow the path up to the trig' point and then along the top of Stanage Edge for 2km, where the stony track known as the Long Causeway cuts across the path. Follow this downhill to join the road below the edge.

**7** **Turn left**, cross a cattle grid and **turn right immediately**. Follow the path alongside the wood on Dennis Knoll. Descend to cottages. **Turn left, then right** and resume the descent along a path, eventually emerging at a road. Cross this and continue along the obvious footpath, which joins a track further on leading back into Hathersage.

*STANAGE EDGE AND HIGGER TOR  PHOTO: JON BARTON*

WIN HILL SUMMIT *PHOTO: MAUREEN POPE*

# 10 Win Hill Pike & Crook Hill

15.1km/9.4miles

A walk with 'Lakeland' character, traversing two broad ridges that form the high ground around Ladybower Reservoir.

Heatherdene » Win Hill Pike » Hope Cross » Hagg Farm » Bridge-end-Pasture » Crook Hill » Heatherdene

## Start

**Heatherdene car park, Ladybower, on the A6013 Ladybower to Bamford road. GR: SK 202859.**

## The Walk

From *Heatherdene*, on the banks of Ladybower Reservoir, we cross the dam and follow a path up into the pine forest. This climbs in stages to the upper edge of the forest, beyond which rears the rocky summit of *Win Hill Pike* (462m). Our route takes a path that contours around the hillside at first, before the Pike has to be reckoned with. There is a choice of paths; both are strenuous, although only for a short distance.

Once on the summit the fabulous views stretching out in all directions can be fully appreciated. A steady descent along the ridge leads to a junction with the Roman Road, a stoney track built by the Roman army to provide a link between Navio, the fort at Brough, and Melandra, the fort at Glossop. After a kilometre, just past *Hope Cross*, this track is forsaken for

another ancient track winding downhill to the Snake Pass and a crossing of the River Ashop.

We now follow its continuation uphill past *Hagg Farm* via steep switchbacks – popular with mountain bikers – to reach a saddle on the long ridge that stretches from Bleaklow to the Ashopton Viaduct at the foot of the Snake Pass. The route follows a bridleway along the ridge and climbs steadily to another superb viewpoint at the summit of *Bridge-end Pasture*.

From here, we follow the bridleway in descent, and then take a short diversion to the twin summits of *Crook Hill* (382m and 374m); prominent gritstone tors that until 2004 were inaccessible to the public. After descending to the viaduct, a gentle kilometre alongside Ladybower Reservoir – with a potential diversion to the Ladybower Inn – leads back to the car park at *Heatherdene*.

---

**WIN HILL PIKE & CROOK HILL**

**DISTANCE:** 15.1KM/9.4MILES » **TOTAL ASCENT:** 565M/1,854FT » **START GR:** SK 202859 » **TIME:** ALLOW 5–5.5 HOURS
**MAP:** OS EXPLORER OL1, THE DARK PEAK, 1:25,000 » **REFRESHMENTS:** LADYBOWER INN, JUST OFF ROUTE ON A57
**NAVIGATION:** STRAIGHTFORWARD.

CROOK HILL SUMMITS PHOTO: MAUREEN POPE

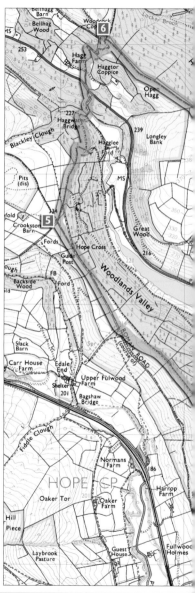

# 10 WIN HILL PIKE & CROOK HILL

# Directions – Win Hill Pike & Crook Hill

➔ From the car park, follow the path past the front of the public toilets. After 500m this leads down to the road opposite the dam. Cross the road and walk across the dam.

**2** **Turn right** and in 150m **turn left** onto the path branching uphill into the forest. After a gate, cross a track and maintain the same course along an old grass track. On reaching another track cross this and go through a gate, hidden from view. Continue on the old, wet track for 400m to where a path branches uphill to the left (signposted *Win Hill*).

**3** **Turn left** onto this path, ignoring any other paths, to emerge on the moor at the top edge of the forest. **Turn left** and walk along the forest edge to a gate. **Either** turn right and climb the narrow path that runs alongside and on the right of the wall. **Or** continue contouring for a further 300m, and then turn right onto the more obvious well-used path. Both lead steeply to the summit of Win Hill.

**4** **Keep straight ahead** just to the left of the crest of the ridge along the gradually descending path. Stay on this, the most obvious highway, for 3km, to where it descends a little to join the Roman Road (a stoney track) before a gate. Go through the gate and follow the Roman Road for 1km, passing the stone guidepost at Hope Cross, to a track crossroads after a gate.

**5** **Bear right** along the descending track. After the first right-hand bend **turn left** onto a path. Descend to a path junction, **bear right** down to a bridge, cross this and then climb steeply to the main road. Cross this and follow the road towards Hagg Farm. **Keep straight ahead** through a gate and up the steep winding track, taking the **right fork** near the top.

**6** **Turn right**. Follow the bridleway along the crest of the ridge. Keep straight ahead at a junction after 800m. The path climbs gently to a high point on Bridge-end Pasture then descends to a bridleway fork.

**7** **Fork right**. Pass through a bridlegate, then **turn left** and cross the field, heading for the ridge of Crook Hill. Climb this to the summit of Crook Hill's western summit. Continue down to the saddle and climb to the lower summit then **bear left** down the hillside to regain the bridleway. Use the waymarked field path and descend to the farm drive, which is crossed. Continue downhill to the road.

**8** **Turn right** at the road, **then left** at the main road to cross the viaduct. Follow the pavement to the next junction and **turn right** to cross a second viaduct and return to the car park.

*DESCENT TO LADYBOWER RESERVOIR* **PHOTO: BARRY POPE**

WINDGATHER ROCKS FROM PYM CHAIR  PHOTO: MAUREEN POPE

# 11 Goyt Valley & the Tors    15.3km/9.5miles

Takes in a forest, a gritstone edge, a moorland ridge and a secluded woodland valley.

Errwood Reservoir » Midshires Way » Taxal Edge » Cats Tor » Shining Tor » Shooter's Clough » Errwood Reservoir

## Start

**Goyt Valley, west of the A5004 Whaley Bridge to Buxton road. Park in the car park on the west side of the Errwood Dam. GR: SK 013756.**

## The Walk

Starting on the banks of *Errwood Reservoir* in the Goyt Valley, we soon embark on a forest track that forms a short section of the *Midshires Way*, a 360km path linking the ancient Ridgeway in Buckinghamshire with the TransPennine Trail at Stockport.

Emerging from the forest we follow an old track as it winds down into a delightful wooded clough. Now the climb begins in earnest, first along a lane through farmland and subsequently on a footpath through heather and bilberry to gain a long escarpment at *Taxal Edge* that develops into a ridge and forms a good half of our walk.

The ascent of the ridge comes in stages. To begin with, we follow the path uphill through pastures to the gritstone crag of Windgather Rocks. The view unfolds to either side revealing the high moors to the east and a deep valley and rolling hills to the west.

The vegetation and terrain take on a bleaker, moorland character as we climb to *Cats Tor*, then to the highest point on the walk at *Shining Tor* (559m). Dominating the view to the southwest is the volcano shaped Shutlingsloe, rising from Wildboarclough. The descent is along an old track that follows a subsidiary ridge back to the Goyt Valley with stunning views of Errwood Reservoir below and the high moors beyond.

A final treat awaits those who follow the less direct, recommended route back via *Shooter's Clough*. A path winds down into an enchanting wooded valley wherein lie the ruins of Errwood Hall, once the seat of the Grimshawes, who prospered during the Industrial Revolution.

## GOYT VALLEY AND THE TORS

**DISTANCE:** 15.3KM/9.5MILES » **TOTAL ASCENT:** 509M/1,670FT » **START GR:** SK 013756 » **TIME:** ALLOW 5 HOURS
**MAP:** OS EXPLORER OL24, THE WHITE PEAK, 1:25,000 » **REFRESHMENTS:** NONE ON ROUTE
**NAVIGATION:** STRAIGHTFORWARD.

**11 GOYT VALLEY &
THE TORS**

# **Directions** – Goyt Valley & the Tors

**❻** Go through the car park to its upper exit and continue up the steep road (or the grass bank on the left) to a gate with a fingerpost for *Hoo Moor* on the right.

**2** **Go through the gate** and follow the forest track. After 2km pass through a gate (footpath to Taxal) and then through a farm. Follow the track, which soon winds downhill, crosses Mill Clough, then climbs past Madscar Farm. Here the track becomes a tarmac lane. Stay on this as it doubles back uphill and bypasses Overton Hall farm and joins a road.

**3** **Cross the road** and take the footpath opposite going straight uphill. After cresting the ridge **cross a stile** and keep a wall on the left. **Cross a stile adjacent to a large tree** then continue to the farmhouse ahead.

**4** Opposite the house cross a stile on the left, then continue with a wall on the right up the ridge to Windgather Rocks. Stay close to the edge of the crag for the view. When the crag relents **keep straight ahead**. Cross a stile in a wall on the right and continue up the road for 1km to a stile on the left.

**5** **Take the left fork** (away from the wall). Follow the footpath for 500m to a road. **Turn right.** Cross the road after a few metres and then a stile. Follow the footpath along the ridge for 3km, up and then down Cats Tor, and onwards up to the trig' point on Shining Tor (just to the right of the footpath, over a stile).

**6** **Bear left downhill** as for the Cat and Fiddle, then uphill to a footpath junction.

**7** **Turn left** and follow the old track signed *Errwood*. This descends a ridge. After 1km turn left* at a gate leading to Errwood Hall and Shooter's Clough. The path winds downhill to a stream crossing then bears right and descends parallel with the stream. Continue to a junction with a track.

**⟳** **\*SC**: Continue straight ahead to return more directly to the car park.

**8** **Turn right**. Follow the track downhill, passing the track leading to the ruins of Errwood Hall. After crossing the river at a bridge, the track climbs a little and bears right. **Keep straight ahead** here along a path down to a car park. **Turn left**, walk alongside the road for 300m, and then use the footpath on the left that parallels the road back to the car park.

THE LOCALS  *PHOTO: MAUREEN POPE*

PANNIERS BRIDGE, THREE SHIRE HEADS  PHOTO: BARRY POPE

# 12 A Walk In Three Shires

16.1km/10miles

Traces a route through deep, winding river valleys and across open moor passing an ancient river crossing where three counties meet.

Clough House » Wildboarclough » Three Shire Heads » Axe Edge Moor » Cat and Fiddle » Clough House

## Start

Old Clough House car park and picnic area, Wildboarclough. 1.6km north of the A54, 10km southwest of Buxton. GR: SJ 987698.

## The Walk

We start our walk in a deep secluded valley flanked by high hills with wooded slopes and tumbling mountain streams. From the picnic area at *Clough House* a path leads down the valley to the scattered settlement of *Wildboarclough*. Here our route passes the village church, built with the red sandstones of Cheshire, and climbs out of the valley on lane, track and footpath and up onto the moor.

An ancient packhorse trail is now followed down into the Dane Valley to Panniers Bridge and *Three Shire Heads*, where Cheshire, Derbyshire and Staffordshire meet. This is a particularly attractive spot and popular with picnickers. The packhorse route is followed up a narrow ravine that snakes up onto *Axe Edge Moor* via track, lane and grassy trail.

We descend to join a track above the Goyt Valley, which in turn descends to the head of the River Goyt at Derbyshire Bridge. Steady climbing leads us up to the *Cat and Fiddle*, the highest pub in the region.

From here, we follow a bridleway across another stretch of moor from which the huge radio telescope at Jodrell Bank can be seen standing proud of the Cheshire Plain. A rapid descent to the car park follows, first down into a rocky gully where the path requires care, then along the stony track of Cumberland Brook, with views across to the jutting peak of Shutlingsloe.

## A WALK IN THREE SHIRES

**DISTANCE:** 16.1KM/10MILES » **TOTAL ASCENT:** 511M/1,677FT » **START GR:** SJ 987698 » **TIME:** ALLOW 5.5 HOURS
**MAP:** OS EXPLORER OL24, THE WHITE PEAK, 1:25,000 » **REFRESHMENTS:** CAT AND FIDDLE ON A537
**NAVIGATION:** STRAIGHTFORWARD.

PHOTO: NORMAN TAYLOR

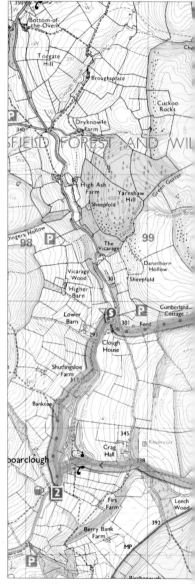

## 12 A WALK IN THREE SHIRES

# **Directions** – A Walk In Three Shires

**◐▸** Walk out of the lower entrance to the car park, **turn left**, follow the road, and in 200m **bear right** along the path to Langley via Shutlingsloe. Follow this above the road, past a cottage, then join a tarmac lane and continue straight on to a road junction.

**2** **Turn left**, and then **turn right** to cross the bridge and follow the road steeply uphill. Pass a junction after 600m and continue uphill to where the road bends right. **Keep straight ahead** up a track as for Three Shire Heads. Pass through a gate then maintain the same course uphill. Pass through a gate then continue to the main road. Cross this and go through the gate opposite. **Keep straight ahead** until a road is reached.

**3** **Turn right**, and then **bear left immediately** through a gate. Follow the track down to Panniers Bridge at Three Shire Heads.

**4** **Cross the bridge, keep straight ahead** through a gate and ascend the rocky bridleway. **Fork left** after 200m. This becomes a tarmac lane as it climbs steeply to a T-junction.

**5** **Turn left**. The tarmac is replaced by a gravel track. **Keep straight ahead** where the track bends sharp left. Pass through a gate and continue along the gradually ascending grassy track with the gully on the right as far as a fork. **Fork left**. This leads over the moor and joins a road.

**6** **Turn right** and, in 50m, **turn left** along the Dane Valley Way (abbreviated on signposts to *DVW*). Follow this downhill to the main road. Cross it and **bear slightly left** to follow the path's continuation. **Cross a stile, keep straight ahead**, and reach a wide track after 800m.

**7** **Turn left**. Follow the track for 1km, descending to the car park at Derbyshire Bridge. **Keep straight ahead** and follow the lane uphill for 1.5km to a junction with the main road. **Turn right** and walk up to the Cat and Fiddle public house.

**8** Cross the road and follow the bridleway opposite the pub across the moor. This climbs gradually then bends to the left. Continue to the public footpath signpost for *Wildboarclough*.

**9** Follow this path downhill. It crosses a stream and further on descends into the rocky gully down which the stream flows. The path joins a track. **Turn right** and follow this downhill, eventually crossing a footbridge and, a little further on, arriving at the road opposite the upper entrance of Clough House car park.

*THREE SHIRE HEADS  PHOTO: BARRY POPE*

# SECTION 3

## Limestone Country

*These walks are located in the central and southern Peak District – the White Peak. They take in spectacular crag-lined limestone gorges with caves, rock pinnacles and scree slopes rich in fossils.*

*They climb to the top of prominent peaks, once submarine reef knolls in a tropical area. They cross limestone upland, with fascinating relics of the lead mining industry; and pass through quaint villages with Norman churches, old stone cottages and inviting inns.*

THE PATH FROM DEEP DALE TO SHELDON (WALK 16)  PHOTO: JOHN COEFIELD

E.R.

ERECTED
TO
COMMEMORATE
THE
CORONATION
OF
KING EDWARD VII
1902.

# 13 Hartington to Longnor

15.9km/9.9miles

Passes through contrasting countryside around the Rivers Manifold and Dove, visiting ancient earthworks en route.

Hartington » Sheen » Brund » Longnor » Crowdecote » Pilsbury Castle » Hartington

## Start

Hartington Market Square. Parking on the square or in the Pay and Display car park. GR: SK 127605.

## The Walk

An important market town in the middle ages, *Hartington* is now a busy village of attractive old cottages, hostelries and novelty shops set around a large market square. Of particular interest is The Old Cheese Shop in the square, which sells stilton from the Hartington Creamery, now part of Dairy Crest.

Leaving the village heading west, we cross the River Dove and the boundary between Derbyshire and Staffordshire. A climb leads us up to a broad ridge and the scattered settlement of *Sheen*.

Continuing west across rolling pastures, we drop down to the secluded hamlet of *Brund* in the wide valley of the River Manifold. We follow a footpath from here upstream above the meandering river through a quintessentially English pastoral landscape.

The climb out of this pleasant valley leads to *Longnor*, a substantial village on the ridge separating the Dove and Manifold Valleys – much quieter than Hartington but no less attractive.

We descend from *Longnor* to cross the River Dove, a stream at this point, and head for the earthwork remains of *Pilsbury Castle*, a Norman motte and bailey built in 1068-69, partly on a reef limestone knoll, which is incorporated into its defences.

We climb out of the valley bottom and, where the path levels out, look back for a stunning view up the valley to the former reef knolls of Chrome Hill and Parkhouse Hill, jagged and mountain-like in appearance. Our route continues at a high level along the valley side with one sharp, grassy climb as we make our way back to *Hartington*.

## HARTINGTON TO LONGNOR

**DISTANCE:** 15.9KM/9.9MILES » **TOTAL ASCENT:** 335M/1,100FT » **START GR:** SK 127605 » **TIME:** ALLOW 5 HOURS
**MAP:** OS EXPLORER OL1 THE WHITE PEAK 1:25,000 » **REFRESHMENTS:** CREWE AND HARPUR ARMS, HORSESHOE INN, CHESHIRE CHEESE P.H. AND CRAFT SHOP CAFÉ IN LONGNOR; CHARLES COTTON HOTEL, DEVONSHIRE ARMS AND TEASHOPS IN HARTINGTON » **NAVIGATION:** STRAIGHTFORWARD.

**13 HARTINGTON TO LONGNOR**

# **Directions** – Hartington to Longnor

**➏▸** From the centre of Hartington, **take the road to the left of The Old Cheese Shop.** Just before reaching the cheese factory **turn right** onto the path to Sheen. Pass through a strip of woodland and **take a diagonal line across a field.** A little further on, the path bears slightly left to descend a shallow gully right of an ash tree then crosses the River Dove by a footbridge. Continue up to and across a track, **then keep straight ahead** up a steep slope as for Sheen. Go through a bridlegate at the top.

**➋** **Keep straight ahead** by the side of the wall, with a little diversion to the right and back, and join a track. Follow this as it bends right then heads up to the farm to emerge at the road in Sheen.

**➌** **Turn right**, and then cross the road to the stile on the left (fingerpost). Follow the path through fields and join a track at a gate with stile. Follow the track, which bends right after 300m and descends to the road in Brund

**➍** **Bear right** and follow the winding road to a junction. **Turn right** and then **left after a few metres** onto the path for Longnor. Keep straight ahead for 600m, where the path meets a meander of the River Manifold. The path now bears right away from the river uphill. Continue along the obvious footpath. **Pass left of a farm**, cross a footbridge, then **keep straight ahead** as for Longnor, keeping a hedge on the right. **Pass left** of more farm buildings and **continue straight ahead**, crossing a track. **Pass left of another farm** (Lower Boothlow) and then **keep straight ahead** with a wall on the right to a stile.

**➎** **Fork left** at the path junction. Follow this above the river for 1km, after which it bears right uphill to reach a stile in the top left-hand corner of the field. Cross this and **bear left** through the farmyard as waymarked. Continue up to the main road in Longnor. *(Village centre, pubs and teashop to the left.)*

**➏** **Cross the road, walk up the lane opposite.** Follow it as it bears right and **take the first narrow lane on the left.** Continue to a T-junction, **turn left** and then **bear right** along the bridleway – a concrete track. Follow this downhill and then follow the bridleway's continuation from the far side of a small barn. **Keep straight ahead**, passing a short boggy section, then a footbridge, and go to a gate with stile.

**7** Cross this and **turn right immediately** to cross another stile. The path becomes a track, which is followed to a road at Crowdecote. **Turn right,** walk to the junction and **turn right again**. Walk past the Packhorse Inn and turn left on a lane/track. Where the track ends, **keep straight ahead** along the obvious path to Pilsbury Castle.

**8** After visiting the motte and bailey **bear left** up a grassy path. Follow this to a road, cross it, and **keep straight ahead** as far as a stile and fingerpost.

**9** **Turn right** as for Hartington, walk steeply uphill and cross a gate and stile. Follow the waymarked path for 2km and join a track at a bend. Walk uphill and through a gate or a stile and stay parallel with the wall on the right. Cross a stile and keep the same course across fields to emerge at a road.

**10** **Turn right**. Follow the road downhill for 250m and **bear right** down a leafy old track into Hartington. **Turn left** to return to the start.

*THE OLD CHEESE SHOP  PHOTO: NORMAN TAYLOR*

BEESTON TOR  PHOTO: JOHN COEFIELD

# 14 Throwley Moor & Grindon

18.1km/11.2 miles

A demanding outing through the dramatic hill and gorge country of the southern Peak.

Wettonmill » Weag's Bridge » Beeston Tor » Mere Hill » Waterfall » Grindon » Butterton » Wettonmill

## Start

Wettonmill in the Manifold Valley, 5km south of Hulme End, which itself is on the B5054 midway between Warslow and Hartington. GR: SK 095561.

## The Walk

Our walk starts deep in the meandering gorge of the Manifold Valley at *Wettonmill*, a pretty riverside spot by an elegant bridge. From here we follow an old and little used road downstream, then join the Manifold Way, the former trackbed of the Leek and Manifold Valley Light Railway. Closed in 1934, it was used to transport milk from farms bordering the valley and also tourists to Thor's Cave, an impressive gaping hole in a towering limestone buttress near Wetton.

After *Weag's Bridge*, our route passes the great cliff of *Beeston Tor*, popular with rock climbers, and then climbs out of the gorge, giving stunning views of the inaccessible lower reaches of the Manifold Valley. Little used field paths are followed up *Mere Hill*, where we can enjoy more extensive views of the local area.

A rapid descent leads us down into the gorge of the River Hamps, more often a dry bed than an abundant flow, where we cross the Manifold Way and climb to *Waterfall*, a hamlet of scattered farms and cottages with a pub.

Passing through *Back o' th' Brook*, a bridleway now leads to *Grindon*, entered in the Domesday Book as *Grendon* (Green Hill). Our route continues through meadows and descends to an attractive ford before climbing steeply to another upland village: *Butterton*, whereafter a footpath through a lovely valley rounds off a very pleasant walk.

## THROWLEY MOOR & GRINDON

**DISTANCE:** 18.1KM/11.2MILES » **TOTAL ASCENT:** 475M/1,558FT » **START GR:** SK 095561 » **TIME:** ALLOW 5.5 HOURS
**MAP:** OS EXPLORER OL24 THE WHITE PEAK 1:25,000 » **REFRESHMENTS:** RED LION P.H. AT WATERFALL; CAVALIER INN AT GRINDON; BLACK LION AT BUTTERTON; NATIONAL TRUST CAFÉ AT WETTONMILL » **NAVIGATION:** STRAIGHTFORWARD.

**14 THROWLEY MOOR & GRINDON**

# **Directions** – Throwley Moor & Grindon

**⟶** Cross the ford (slippery) opposite the bridge or use the footbridge. Follow the old road for 500m and then **bear right** at the junction across the old railway bridge to follow the Manifold Way. Continue for 2.5km to a road crossing at Weag's Bridge. Cross the road and **keep straight ahead** along the left-hand lane. Cross a bridge and walk as far as a cottage.

**2** **Bear right** up the bridleway to Throwley. The track ends at a gate. Stay parallel with the fence on the right and ascend to a wall ahead. **Turn left**, then ignore the footpath sign and **bear right** with the same wall (path with public access). Cross two stiles/gateways and then **bear half right** for 200m before swinging left towards the right-hand end of the remains of a wall. **Keep straight ahead** without losing height, passing through a gate, and aim for the right edge of the wood ahead, where a road is joined.

**3** **Bear right** along the road. After crossing a cattle grid cross the stile on the right just beyond a track. Descend to the River Hamps (often dry riverbed).

**4** Cross a footbridge and the Manifold Way and the gate opposite. Continue up the valley alongside the stream and cross a slab footbridge after 800m. Climb the stile – **not** the gate – and **bear half right** up the field (**no path**). Aim for a stile/gateway between a farm and prominent house. Continue to the road in Waterfall.

**5** **Turn left and then right** at the junction. **Turn right** at the second road at the left-hand bend. Pass the Red Lion and follow the lane downhill. **Bear right** at a junction and follow the lane round a right-hand bend, past a pond, to a sharp right-hand bend.

**6** **Turn left**, and then **keep straight ahead** and through a gate. Follow the bridleway uphill. Where the track ends stay with the fence on the right. Upon reaching a farm, pass through the farmyard and follow the lane to a junction at Grindon.

**7**  Turn left, and then take the next road right towards the church. **Bear left** to the picnic area, **cross a stile on the left** here, then keep a hedge on the left. After several fields **bear half right** down a field, as waymarked. Cross a stile then ascend to the back of a barn (boggy). **Turn left** and pass between farm buildings, then join a road. Cross the road and a stile, and then another in 30m and **continue straight ahead**. After 400m join a road by a gate on the left.

**8**  **Bear right**. Follow the road downhill to the ford and the walkway, and continue steeply uphill into Butterton. Pass the inn, follow the road right, and then turn right at a junction 300m further on. Continue along the road for 1km to a bridleway sign and gateway on the right.

**9**  **Turn right. Keep straight ahead** and descend steeply to a path junction before a footbridge. **Turn left** and walk above the brook back to Wettonmill.

*BUTTERTON PHOTO: JOHN COEFIELD*

RIVER WYE WEIR AT CRESSBROOK  PHOTO: JOHN COEFIELD

# 15 Miller's Dale & Monsal Dale

17.6km/11 miles

A combination of limestone upland and a deep, cliff-lined river gorge with plenty of industrial archaeology.

Miller's Dale » Blackwell » Priestcliffe » High Dale » Monsal Dale » Monsal Head » Cressbrook » Litton Mill » Miller's Dale

## Start

Former railway station at Miller's Dale, just off the B6049. GR: SK 138733.

## The Walk

From the former railway station at *Miller's Dale* we follow the River Wye up Chee Dale for a short distance, before climbing out of the valley up a steep grassy hillside. Where this eases off, a close look at the terrain to the right of the path reveals hummocky ground that is the hut circle remains of an ancient settlement.

Continuing the climb through upland pastures our route leads to the hamlet of *Blackwell*. A mile of road walking along a quiet lane takes us through the scattered hamlet of *Priestcliffe*, from where an old walled track is followed above *High Dale*. This is forsaken for a woodland path that leads down to *Monsal Dale*.

The riverside path is followed to the footbridge and weir, before a climb leads to *Monsal Head*, where refreshments could be taken at either the café or pub.

We then descend to Monsal Viaduct and follow the Monsal Trail as far as *Cressbrook*. The former textile mill – that has recently undergone conversion to luxury apartments – was established by Sir Richard Arkwright in the 18th century.

After passing over the tumbling waters of the gorge below the millpond, we follow the riverside path through the limestone gorge of the beautifully named Water-cum-Jolly. This leads to *Litton Mill*, another 18th century textile mill that has undergone modern conversion. Coot, moorhen, dabchicks and mallard are amongst the wildlife that babble around amongst the reeds along this section.

From *Litton Mill* there is a choice of routes. Either pick up the Monsal Trail and follow this back to *Miller's Dale*, or follow the more interesting quiet road alongside the river as far as the Angler's Rest before rejoining the Trail.

---

## MILLER'S DALE & MONSAL DALE

**DISTANCE:** 17.6KM/11MILES » **TOTAL ASCENT:** 600M/1,969FT » **START GR:** SK 138733 » **TIME:** ALLOW 5.5-6 HOURS
**MAP:** OS EXPLORER OL24 THE WHITE PEAK 1:25,000 » **REFRESHMENTS:** PUB AND CAFÉ AT MONSAL HEAD; ANGLER'S REST AT MILLER'S DALE NEAR THE END OF THE WALK » **NAVIGATION:** STRAIGHTFORWARD ON WELL-USED PATHS AND TRACKS.

### 15 MILLER'S DALE & MONSAL DALE

# **Directions** – Miller's Dale & Monsal Dale

➲ Walk to the front of the former station building and **turn right** onto the former railway track bed. Continue to the bridge before the blocked-off tunnel and **turn right** to descend to the riverside path. **Turn right** and walk upstream to the footbridge – the first 200m require caution where the path slopes toward the river.

**2** Cross the footbridge, **bear left** at first, then head up the steep grassy hillside taking the easiest line. The path straightens out as the slope relents. Cross a stile and keep a wall on the right. On reaching the start of a track, **follow this right, and then left** up to Blackwell Hall Farm. Stay on the farm drive, which leads to the road in Blackwell.

**3** **Turn left** and continue down to a junction. Cross the main road and continue **straight ahead**. Pass through Priestcliffe Ditch and ascend to a road junction.

**4** **Turn left** and follow the road to a hairpin bend. **Keep straight ahead** along a track for 100m, **fork right and then left almost immediately**. Follow the walled track for just under 3km to the cottages at Brushfield.

**5** **Turn left**. Follow the track past the front of the cottages and through a gate. Continue on the high level track for about 1km to level ground. There is a break in the track at this point and a path goes right down to Brushfield Hough Farm.

**6** Take this path to and through the farm and then follow a track to a right-hand bend. Cross a stile in the wall straight ahead and continue down through woods to a junction with the path running through Monsal Dale.

**7** **Turn left**, walk up Monsal Dale, cross the river at the footbridge before the weir and ascend to Monsal Head*. The route from here takes the path down to the Monsal Viaduct (signposted).

➲ **\*SC: Or** continue by the river and pass under the viaduct. Carry on past a footbridge and ascend to the Monsal Trail at point 8.

**8** Follow the Monsal Trail to a blocked-off tunnel, where a **footpath right** takes you down to a river crossing just below the millpond at Cressbrook. **Turn left** and take the riverside path upstream below steep cliffs. Continue to Litton Mill.

**9** At Litton Mill there is a choice of routes.

> After passing through the former mill **either turn left** opposite cottages to cross the river by a footbridge, ascend to the Monsal Trail then turn right to follow this back to Miller's Dale.

**Or, our recommended route,** walk alongside the river on the quiet lane as far as the Angler's Rest, then cross the river at this point and ascend to the Trail, **turning right** to finish.

*OLD MILL WORKINGS, CRESSBROOK PHOTO JOHN COEFIELD*

# 16 An Upland Village Trail

17.1km/10.6miles

A walk across rolling limestone upland passing through five White Peak villages and the impressive ruins of Magpie Mine.

Taddington » Deep Dale » Sheldon » Magpie Mine » Monyash » Flagg » Chelmorton » Taddington

## Start

Taddington, just off the A6 between Buxton and Bakewell. The walk is described from the church at the north end of the village. Roadside parking. GR: SK 142711.

## The Walk

Starting at the top end of *Taddington*, we walk down the street past limestone cottages of all shapes and sizes, as well as farms, barns, and a tiny chapel. Our route out of the village uses old walled tracks that have degenerated into footpaths since the decline in use of horse-drawn vehicles.

Further on, we descend a steep grass slope into *Deep Dale*, which hosts a spectacular display of purple orchid and cowslip during May and early June. An equally steep grass slope has to be climbed to vacate the dale but this is short, and the path continues more easily across fields to *Sheldon*, an upland village of former lead miners' cottages and farms. Our next objective is nearby *Magpie Mine*, whose impressive ruins stand as a reminder of the importance of the lead mining industry hereabouts in past centuries.

We continue across rolling meadows and descend to the village of *Monyash*. At roughly the halfway point of our walk, the café and pub, facing the village green, are well placed to fulfil refreshment needs.

We now follow the Limestone Way along old tracks to *Flagg*, a windswept village comprising a few cottages and farms with a chapel and a primary school. A further kilometre of meadow crossing leads us gently down to *Chelmorton*. The route taken overlooks the village and provides a good view of its location within a mesh of narrow fields that hark back to medieval farming methods. Another short, sharp climb past the church leads up to the high ground once more, whence field upon field are crossed as we head back to *Taddington*.

Before the final descent, the efforts of the walk are rewarded with a breathtaking view to the north.

---

## AN UPLAND VILLAGE TRAIL

**DISTANCE:** 17.1KM/10.6MILES » **TOTAL ASCENT:** 359M/1,180FT » **START GR:** SK 142711 » **TIME:** ALLOW 5-5.5 HOURS
**MAP:** OS EXPLORER OL24 WHITE PEAK AREA 1:25,000 » **REFRESHMENTS:** QUEEN ANNE AT TADDINGTON; COCK AND PULLET AT SHELDON; PLOUGH INN AT FLAGG; CAFÉ AND BULL'S HEAD AT MONYASH; CHURCH INN AT CHELMORTON
**NAVIGATION:** STRAIGHTFORWARD IN ALL BUT MISTY CONDITIONS, WHEN STILE SPOTTING CAN BECOME TRICKY.

**16 AN UPLAND VILLAGE TRAIL**

# **Directions** – An Upland Village Trail

**❺▸** Walk down through the village and **fork right** at Town End as far as One Day Cottage. Just beyond, **turn right** on the walled path and then **bear left** off this after 100m to follow another walled path. On reaching the T-junction **turn left** and continue to a lane.

**2** **Turn right**. Follow the lane past Over Wheal Farm. 100m beyond a large, in-situ muddy puddle in the track (avoidable on the right), go through the **gate on the left** (with fingerpost). **Bear half right** down to the field corner (no path in evidence), cross the remains of a stile and continue on the same course down the steep grass slope to the footpath in Deep Dale.

**3** Cross the stone stile and climb the steep grass slope opposite, now on a well-used path. After a stile at the top **continue straight ahead** through fields with gateways and then **cross a stile on the left** and resume the former course to join a road via a stile to the left of a gate.

**4** **Turn left**. Walk into Sheldon. Descend through the village to a stile and fingerpost on the right, 150m beyond the Cock and Pullet by The Byre. **Cross this** and keep a straight course through paddocks, letting stiles guide the way until a fingerpost is reached.

**5** **Turn left** to cross the stile and continue to Magpie Mine. Descend steps behind the engine house ruin then **turn right**. Continue across a stile with fingerpost and keep to the obvious footpath to emerge at a road at a stile by a gate.

**6** **Turn right**. Follow the road uphill, past a junction and **cross a stile on the left**. Walk along the field edge to, and through, a copse, and then continue with a wall on the right. **Bear slightly left to a stile after three fields**, and then resume the former course for three fields before **bearing half left** to a stile left of a gate. **Turn right** along the road and follow this down to a T-junction in Monyash.

**7** **Turn left**, walk up the road and **take the walled path on the right before Sheldon House**. *(For the pub and café keep straight on, then retrace your steps.)* After 200m **bear right** along a footpath and follow this to join a track. **Turn right. Keep straight ahead** and pass farm buildings and a derelict barn.

**8**    At the track junction just beyond the barn **bear left** (Limestone Way). Stiles and fingerposts mark the way and lead to a junction with a farm track. **Keep straight ahead**, emerging at a road. **Continue straight ahead** along this. Follow the road to a junction and **turn left**. Walk up through Flagg to a junction.

**9**    **Turn left** and continue to High Stool Farm on the bend. **Turn right**, cross the stile by a gate and then **bear left**. Follow the path for 1km across several fields and up to a road.

**10**    **Turn left and take the second road on the right**. Continue downhill to a junction in Chelmorton.

**11**    **Turn right**. Walk uphill past the pub and church, **bear right** and follow the bridleway steeply uphill. Upon reaching level ground **stay on the right** to join a track at a bridlegate. Cross the track and the stile opposite and **keep straight ahead**. Cross another track and **keep straight ahead**, passing just right of the reservoir at Sough Top. The path now bears slightly right and descends to a road. Cross this and continue downhill into the village.

*DEEP DALE  PHOTO: JOHN COEFIELD*

FOOTPATH

# 17 Around Dove Dale

18.5km/11.5miles

A demanding walk, covering steep ground with stunning views of the hills and valleys around Dove Dale.

Milldale » Thorpe » Bunster Hill » Wetton » Alstonefield » Milldale

## Start

Milldale, 2.5km west off the A515, 8km north of Ashbourne. GR: SK 136547.

## The Walk

From the pretty hamlet of *Milldale* we cross the River Dove by an ancient packhorse bridge and climb out of the gorge by a path that zigzags up the steep valley side. This soon relents to become a more gradual climb to the high pastures above Dove Dale, from where one can appreciate the unfolding panorama.

Our route passes an old limekiln and descends to a pleasant, gated road. We pass through *Thorpe Pasture*, an area of access land stretching into Dove Dale. The Limestone Way is now followed down to the very attractive village of *Thorpe* where after the descent continues more steeply to a crossing of the River Dove; views stunning en route.

A couple of often-muddy fields near the Izaak Walton Hotel have to be negotiated, then we escape to the fine ridge of *Bunster Hill*.

Once attained, the views to either side provide sufficient reward for the effort. The narrow and eroded footpath leading off the other side of the ridge demands care when traversing a steep slope. Trekking poles would be an advantage here.

The climb continues through fields and along ancient tracks and lanes to reach the village of *Wetton*. Our route first descends, and then climbs again to *Alstonefield*. Both villages are attractive settlements of old stone cottages and farms, each with a fine hostelry. Another old lane provides us with a leisurely downhill stroll back to *Milldale*, where refreshments await at Polly's Cottage.

## AROUND DOVE DALE

**DISTANCE:** 18.5KM/11.5MILES » **TOTAL ASCENT:** 544M/1,780FT » **START GR:** SK 136547 » **TIME:** ALLOW 6 HOURS
**MAP:** OS EXPLORER OL24 THE WHITE PEAK 1:25,000 » **REFRESHMENTS:** POLLY'S COTTAGE, MILLDALE; PEVERIL OF THE PEAK HOTEL, THORPE; IZAAK WALTON HOTEL, DOVEDALE; ROYAL OAK, WETTON; THE GEORGE, ALSTONEFIELD
**NAVIGATION:** PATHS ACROSS SEVERAL FIELDS ARE ILL DEFINED BUT STILES AND POSTS HELP NAVIGATION.

CONTINUES ON PAGE 113

**17 AROUND DOVE DALE**

PHOTO: JON BARTON

**17 AROUND DOVE DALE**

# Directions – Around Dove Dale

**➏** Walk down the road into Milldale, **bear right** and cross the River Dove by the old packhorse bridge, then **bear left** immediately up the zigzag path. After the short, steep section follow the more obvious right fork alongside the wall on the right. Continue uphill through a gate, and keep the wall on your right. Eventually a track is reached.

**2** Cross this and continue as for Tissington (fingerpost) along a field track. Pass left of a wood and through a gateway. Keep to the wall on the left to a fingerpost.

**3** **Bear right** here to a gateway *(ignoring the one straight ahead)*. Continue across a stile then join a track. Follow this through the farm and **keep straight ahead** through a stile on the left of a gate. Follow the obvious path through fields, and downhill to join a track. **Bear left** along this to join a road at a gate with stile.

**4** **Turn right**. Follow the road downhill through Thorpe Pasture to a fingerpost and stile on the right for Thorpe (Limestone Way). **Turn right here**. Continue through a gateway then **bear right** to a squeeze stile. Continue downhill keeping a hedge on your left. Cross a stile, go through a gate, and then continue with a wall on your left to a stile/fingerpost. Cross this and continue to the road in Thorpe.

**5** **Turn right**, walk down to the bend, then cross the road to follow a lane up to a junction adjacent to the church. **Bear right**, continue round a right-hand bend and **turn left** along an unmade road. Follow this for 150m and **cross a stile on the right** by a gate. Continue parallel with the wall on the right, and then **keep straight ahead** downhill to a stile. Cross this and descend the steep grass slope to reach the road ahead.

**6** Follow the road downhill, across the River Dove and **turn right** for Dovedale.

> **OR** If visiting the Izaak Walton Hotel use the drive to reach the stile just beyond the front of the building, then turn left.

Otherwise walk up the lane as far as Dovedale Car Park and cross the stile on the left. Cross another stile and follow the path towards the hotel. (Ignore the stile to the hotel.)

**7**    Continue across two stiles and then **take a right fork**. This leads via stiles to a notch in the ridge of Bunster Hill ahead. **Bear right** and continue with care across the steep slope. Continue through a gate. Ascend to a stile then **bear half right**. Keep straight on to join a road.

**8**    **Turn right**. Follow the road for 1km, first uphill, then down to a gate on the left.

**9**    Cross the field diagonally and exit by a gate. **Turn right** (often muddy) and pass through a stile. **Continue straight ahead** keeping a wall on your right. Eventually this joins a track/lane. Follow this uphill then down to and across another lane and continue to Wetton. **Keep straight ahead** as far as the Royal Oak pub.

**10**    **Turn right** and follow the road to the second junction, then pass through a gate next to a gate on the right. Descend the field diagonally, pass through another gate and continue as waymarked to a stile and track. **Turn right**. Follow the track to a road.

**11**    **Turn left**. Follow the road for 500m to a gate on the left opposite another gate on the right. **Turn left**. Follow the path uphill to cottages in Alstonefield.

**12**    **Turn right**. Follow the main road, bearing left, then turn right in front of The George pub. **Continue straight ahead**, pass the church and descend to Milldale on the lane. **Turn right** to finish.

PHOTO: JON BARTON

# 18 Robin Hood's Stride from Youlgreave

17.6km/10.9miles

Passes through limestone dales and gritstone hill country with craggy tors in a secluded enclave of the National Park.

Youlgreave » Bradford Dale » Long Dale » Elton » Limestone Way » Robin Hood's Stride » Alport » Youlgreave

## Start

**Youlgreave car park, western edge of the village. GR: SK 205641.**

## The Walk

*Youlgreave*, our starting point, is a fine ancient village whose growth owes much to the rich veins of lead mined in the area over centuries gone by. Indeed 'Youlgreave' derives from 'Auld Grove', or 'Old Mine'.

From the village we descend to *Bradford Dale* and follow the riverside path upstream past several weirs. Waterfowl dabble in the pools and herons are frequently seen along this steep-sided, wooded valley.

Where the dale peters out, our route crosses meadows and passes through the enchanting little gorge of Rusden Wood, afterwards climbing gradually through upland pastures. Suddenly, the sweeping curves of the deep and narrow *Long Dale* are revealed. We pass through this secluded valley and strike out into open country.

After descending to the village of *Elton*, a path is followed across hillside pasture from where there is a clear view of the gritstone tor of *Robin Hood's Stride*. The twin towers resemble the chimneys of a large hall from this angle, hence its other name, 'Mock Beggars Hall'.

We join the *Limestone Way* for the ascent to the *Stride*, from where a short diversion can be made to the 12th century Hermit's Cave at the foot of Cratcliffe Tor.

The route now descends to *Alport* on the River Bradford, a hamlet of pretty cottages with a little humpback bridge and a weir. We follow the river up the little dale then climb back to *Youlgreave*.

## ROBIN HOOD'S STRIDE FROM YOULGREAVE

**DISTANCE:** 17.6KM/10.9MILES » **TOTAL ASCENT:** 494M/1,620FT » **START GR:** SK 205641 » **TIME:** ALLOW 5–5.5 HOURS **MAP:** OS EXPLORER OL24 THE WHITE PEAK 1:25,000 » **REFRESHMENTS:** CAFÉ AND THE CROWN IN ELTON; THE FARMYARD INN, THE BULLS HEAD AND THE GEORGE IN YOULGREAVE » **NAVIGATION:** STRAIGHTFORWARD.

**18 ROBIN HOOD'S STRIDE FROM YOULGREAVE**

# **Directions** – Robin Hood's Stride from Youlgreave

**↪** **Turn left** out of the car park, walk down the road to the Methodist Chapel, and **turn right** onto Bankside. Descend to the river, cross the footbridge, **turn right** and follow the riverside path up the dale. Stay on the left (south) side of the river. The path eventually crosses the river in its upper reaches.

**2** Instead of leaving the dale along the ascending path **turn left** along a narrow footpath (now briefly on the right (west) of the river). Cross the river again by a footbridge then climb an iron staircase and **bear right**. Follow the path and **bear right** to cross a stone slab footbridge with inscription. **Keep straight ahead** through fields with stiles to emerge at a track.

**3** Cross the track and the stile opposite and walk on the right (north) of a stream. Pass through a gate into Rusden Wood and follow the path up the little dry gorge. **Fork left** to cross a stile and continue to a road.

**4** **Turn left**. Continue up the road to a sharp left-hand bend but **keep straight ahead** up a bridleway. This climbs gradually and after 1km passes through a gate **on the right** and makes a right kink before resuming the former course. Continue to a point above a prominent narrow valley immediately after passing through a gate.

**5** **Bear slightly left** and descend into Long Dale. Follow the path through the dale to a path junction. To the left is Gratton Dale. **Turn right** here and follow the bridleway up to a main road.

**6** **Turn left**, walk along the grass verge for 200m, and then **bear left** through a gate (fingerpost) by the junction. Follow the path in a straight line, across fields linked by stiles. After 1.5km the path joins a track. Follow this down to a track junction, and **bear right. Keep straight ahead**, emerging at a road.

**7** **Turn left**. Walk down to the main junction in Elton. Cross the road and then the stile with a fingerpost, and walk through the graveyard. Cross a back lane and a stile on the right of a cottage. Keep straight ahead. **Where the path becomes ambiguous stay high**, then head for a stile to emerge at a lane.

**8** **Turn left**. Follow the lane downhill to the bend, and then go through the gate straight ahead (Limestone Way). Continue up the track and **keep straight ahead** uphill where this bends right to cottages. With Robin Hood's Stride to the left, cross the stile on the left, then another on the right in a few metres. Follow the obvious path to a lane.

**9** **Turn right**. Walk down the lane. Take the bridleway option opposite the Limestone Way path. Rejoin the lane and continue for another 400m.

**10** Turn left through a bridgelate. Continue through a field and join a lane above cottages. **Turn left** and walk down the lane for 500m to a crossroads with a track. **Turn right**, follow the track up to a farm and **keep straight ahead** down the farm drive to join a road.

**11** **Turn left**. Follow the road downhill and cross the bridge into Alport. **Turn left** at the first road, and continue to a junction with the main road.

**12** Pass through the gate on the left and follow the riverside path upstream through the dale to a road. Cross this, continue a little further alongside the river, then **bear right** up a tarmac path into Youlgreave. **Turn left** at the main road to finish.

PHOTO: JOHN COEFIELD

MEADOWLAND ON TIDESWELL MOOR  PHOTO: JON BARTON

# 19 Tideswell Moor & The Hucklows    15.6km/9.7miles

Takes in the rolling limestone landscape north of Tideswell, four White Peak villages, and includes a path with superb views of a limestone dale.

Tideswell » Little Hucklow » Great Hucklow » Grindlow » Wardlow Mires » Litton » Tideswell

## Start

Tideswell. Parking areas beside Tideswell Church, in Cherry Tree Square near the public toilets and opposite the small Catholic Church on the main road. The walk is described from Cherry Tree Square. GR: SK 151755.

## The Walk

*Tideswell* has a very grand 14th century church – the Church of St John the Baptist – known as the Cathedral of the Peak. It was built on the wealth created when the village was the centre of the wool trade and lead mining in the region, the latter very much in evidence on this route

Climbing out of *Tideswell* an old walled track and a short section of road walking take us out onto Tideswell Moor. Our path follows a worked-out lead rake – or mineral vein – up and over Tides Low with good views of the area, and then descends to *Little Hucklow*, a cluster of limestone cottages with a chapel and a very old inn.

From *Little Hucklow* we descend along a lane and then follow a track uphill into *Great Hucklow* which, as its name suggests, is a larger village than it's neighbour. The walk continues through nearby *Grindlow*, the third but not the last '–low' encountered. The word is of Saxon origin, denoting a heaped structure, often a Bronze Age burial mound or barrow.

Tracks and field paths lead us downhill to *Wardlow Mires*, where you could step back in time with a visit to the Three Stags' Heads public house. Opposite the inn is Cressbrook Dale and the distinctive limestone tower known as Peter's Stone. We take a path that climbs at first, and then runs along the rim of the steep valley side offering a sensational view of the dale. The path eventually makes its way through an amazing network of small, walled fields as it enters *Litton*, a fine village of farms, cottages and an inn facing a village green whose centrepiece is a medieval market cross. From *Litton* a quiet lane is followed back to *Tideswell*.

## TIDESWELL MOOR & THE HUCKLOWS

**DISTANCE:** 15.6KM/9.7MILES » **TOTAL ASCENT:** 383M/1,257FT » **START GR:** SK 151755 » **TIME:** ALLOW 5 HOURS
**MAP:** OS EXPLORER OL 1, THE DARK PEAK AND EXPLORER OL 24, THE WHITE PEAK (BOTH 1:25,000) » **REFRESHMENTS:**
BULL'S HEAD AT LITTLE HUCKLOW; QUEEN ANNE AT GREAT HUCKLOW; THREE STAGS' HEADS AT WARDLOW MIRES; RED LION
AT LITTON; SEVERAL PUBS AND A TEASHOP IN TIDESWELL » **NAVIGATION:** STRAIGHTFORWARD.

*EARLY PURPLE ORCHID PHOTO: JOHN COEFIELD*

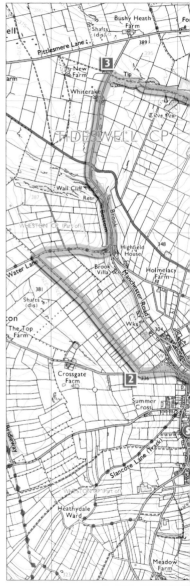

# 19 TIDESWELL MOOR & THE HUCKLOWS

# Directions – Tideswell Moor & The Hucklows

**➒** With your back to Cherry Tree Square **turn left**. Walk through the village, **forking left** for Wheston. Continue for 500m and then **turn left** on the road to Wheston. **Almost immediately** leave the road to follow a path uphill beside a copse, rejoining the same road further on. Continue to a track on the right.

**2** **Turn right** onto this and follow it for 1km to a T-junction. **Turn right** here. Descend the track to a road. **Turn left** and follow the road to a junction. Cross the main road with care and continue uphill along a narrow lane.

**3** After passing cottages **turn right** at a stile with a fingerpost. Head for another stile with a fingerpost on the right in 250m. Continue around a former spoil heap, cross a stile and **keep straight ahead** uphill, to the right of the old lead mine rake. Pass the TV mast and continue, now in descent, with the wall still to your right. The path joins a road.

**4** **Turn left** and walk along the road. About 100m beyond a junction cross either a cattle grid or stile to the right. Follow the track towards cottages in Little Hucklow, **bearing left** rather than taking the old walled track behind buildings. On joining the road in the village, **turn right**. Continue downhill past the Bull's Head to a road junction. Cross the main road and follow the track opposite. This descends at first, and then climbs to join the road in Great Hucklow.

**5** **Turn left**. Walk through the village and **take the second road on the right**. Follow this through nearby Grindlow and continue to a T-junction. Cross the road and **keep left of a cottage**. Continue to a track junction.

**6** **Turn right**. Follow the track to Stanley House. Cross the stile on the left at the right-hand bend, and **fork right** down the field. Continue with a wall on the right and pass through a farmyard to emerge at the main road at Wardlow Mires.

**7** Cross the main road (A623) and **turn right**. Cross the road that runs south to Wardlow and continue to a stile on the left, adjacent to a layby. Take the path that heads uphill, not the one heading into the valley bottom. Continue uphill for 700m and then take the concession footpath that clings to the top of the steep slope overlooking Cressbrook Dale. After a further 600m the path bends right above Tansley Dale. It eventually joins the path climbing out of the dale. Follow this via stiles to a track. **Turn left** and then cross the stile on the right and continue into Litton.

**8** **Turn left**. Walk through the village. **Bear left** with the main road, using a pavement on the left when it appears. This descends into Litton Dale. 200m beyond the edge of the village **bear right** adjacent to a solitary cottage, along a lane deemed unsuitable for motor traffic, and follow this back into Tideswell.

*FARMSTEAD ABOVE GREAT HUCKLOW* **PHOTO:** *JON BARTON*

MONSAL DALE FROM MONSAL HEAD  PHOTO: JOHN COEFIELD

# 20 West of Bakewell

16.6km/10.3miles

A demanding but rewarding outing, that takes in the high ground on both sides of the Wye Valley, west of Bakewell.

Bakewell » Sheldon » Great Shacklow Wood » Monsal Dale » Monsal Head » Little Longstone » Great Longstone » Bakewell

## Start

**Numerous car parks in Bakewell. The walk is described from the roundabout in the centre of the town, where the A619 meets the A6. GR: SK 217684**

## The Walk

*Bakewell*, the Peak District's largest town, is a busy but attractive tourist centre located on the River Wye. The town does not rely solely on tourism and has a large livestock market that is held on Mondays. This draws in farmers from around the region and is an event worth experiencing.

Our route climbs steadily out of *Bakewell* through hillside pastures and along quiet lanes to the upland village of *Sheldon*. Entered in the Domesday Book as Schelhadun, the village developed as a farming and lead mining community. Just south of *Sheldon* are the ruins of Magpie Mine; its chimneys and engine house a landmark in the area.

From Sheldon we descend into Great *Shacklow Wood*, which clings to the steep rocky slopes

of the gorge formed by the River Wye. The path descends gradually to begin with, although it is narrow and demands care, and then continues down what initially appears to be a never-ending staircase. No sooner have we reached level ground than we climb back into the wood. Another descent takes us to *Monsal Dale*, with a short, awkward section where path and stream contend for the same limited space.

We climb again, now through woodland, to a high level track above *Monsal Dale*, hard work rewarded by expansive views of the dale. The track descends to the Monsal Trail, crosses the Monsal Viaduct, and climbs to the viewpoint at *Monsal Head*, where refreshments in various forms are well received.

Adequately refuelled, gentle walking leads from *Monsal Head* to *Little Longstone*, and then onto *Great Longstone*, after which footpaths and tracks are followed across upland pasture back to *Bakewell*.

## WEST OF BAKEWELL

**DISTANCE:** 16.6KM/10.3MILES » **TOTAL ASCENT:** 628M/2,060FT » **START GR:** SK 217684 » **TIME:** ALLOW 5.5–6 HOURS
**MAP:** OS EXPLORER OL24 THE WHITE PEAK 1:25,000 » **REFRESHMENTS:** COCK AND PULLET IN SHELDON; STABLES BAR AND CAFÉ IN MONSAL HEAD; PACKHORSE INN IN LITTLE LONGSTONE; WHITE LION AND CRISPIN IN GREAT LONGSTONE
**NAVIGATION:** STRAIGHTFORWARD.

**20 WEST OF BAKEWELL**

# **Directions** – West of Bakewell

**❺** From the roundabout walk up King Street by the Rutland Arms (the B5055 to Monyash). Continue uphill for 250m to a point where the road bends left; **turn right** here down the narrow lane on the right, a few metres past a footpath sign. After a further few metres **turn left** up Parsonage Croft, opposite the church gate. **Keep straight ahead** along the walled public footpath. Continue across fields and cross a road to follow the path's continuation. After a sharp descent climb to a stile, keeping a wall on your left. Cross another road (Crowhill Lane) and follow the obvious path across fields to emerge at a road. (All the stiles are in place but sometimes well camouflaged by vegetation.)

**2** Follow the road for 800m to a sharp right-hand bend. **Bear left** through a gate (fingerpost) to a farm, pass this on the right and then keep straight ahead, eventually descending to the left to a gate. **Turn left** and follow the road to a junction. **Turn left** and then **turn right** at the next junction up into Sheldon.

**3** Just before the Cock and Pullet in Sheldon centre, **turn right** along the track for Sheldon Parish Church. **Keep straight ahead** along this, and then its continuation as a grass track as far as a gate and finger post.

**4** **Turn right** and leave the track to follow a footpath, which descends and crosses a leafy gully. Continue on the same course with a wall on your right. The path enters Great Shacklow Wood by a gate. Follow the narrow path with care as it descends gradually at first, and then descend steps to a junction with another path.

**5** **Turn left**. The path climbs, levels out and then descends steeply to a gate. Care is needed over this short descent. Continue descending and take the path signposted *White Lodge* (picnic area and car park). Cross a stile and pick the best line over a rocky section that forms part of a stream in wet weather. Continue to the car park.

**6** Cross the car park and descend to the main road. Cross this and the stile opposite. Follow the path across another stile and **bear left** for Brushfield. The path climbs steeply through the wood. Cross the stile at the top and **bear right** along a farm track. Pass through the gate as directed and follow the track right alongside the back of a barn. Pass through a gate and **bear right** after the next gateway to join a track after passing through a gate.

**7** Follow the track for 1km, first on the level, and then in descent as far as a sharp left-hand bend. **Keep straight ahead** here along the public bridleway. Join the Monsal Trail at the viaduct. Cross this and take the path up to Monsal Head.

**8** Pass in front of the Monsal Head Hotel, cross the main road and keep straight ahead along the pavement into Little Longstone. Where the pavement ends **take the stile on the right** (left of the gates), and then **bear left** to take the ascending footpath for Great Longstone. The path crosses several fields and a track and emerges at a road in the village.

**9** **Turn left.** Follow the road to a junction and **turn right**. Walk through the village. After the road bends right, **fork left** up Mires Lane and follow this to a junction.

**10** **Turn left**, and then turn right down the path behind Buskey Cottage. After the second stile keep the wall on your right. Cross another stile and maintain the same course down a large field, exiting this by a stile by a gate to the right of a cottage. **Turn left**, and then cross the road to Toll Bar Cottage and take the path opposite. Continue across the Monsal Trail. Follow the bridleway across rolling terrain and downhill into Bakewell. **Turn left** upon joining a road, and then **turn right** down the first public footpath to follow the riverside path to Bakewell Bridge.

*BAKEWELL BRIDGE PHOTO: JOHN COEFIELD*

# Appendix

The following is a list of Tourist Information
Centres, shops, cafes, pubs, websites and other
contacts that might come in handy.

## Tourist Information Centres

www.visitpeakdistrict.com – Official tourism
website for the Peak District & Derbyshire.
www.peakdistrict.org – Official website of the
Peak District National Park Authority.

| | |
|---|---|
| Ashbourne | T: 01335 343 666 |
| Bakewell | T: 01629 816 558 |
| Buxton | T: 01298 25 106 |
| Castleton | T: 01629 816 558 |
| Edale | T: 01433 670 207 |
| Fairholmes, | |
| Upper Derwent Valley | T: 01433 650 953 |
| Glossop | T: 01457 869 176 |
| Manifold Valley | |
| (nr Hartington) | T: 01298 84 679 |
| Matlock | T: 01629 583 388 |

## Food and Drink
### Cafes

(See individual routes for recommendations.)

**The Bakewell Pudding Parlour,** Bakewell

T: 01629 815 107

| | |
|---|---|
| Cottage Café, Castleton | T: 01433 670 293 |
| Edale Cottage Café, Edale | T: 01433 670 293 |
| Elton Café, Elton | T: 01629 650 217 |

**Hobb's Café** (Monsal Head Tea Room)

T: 01629 640 346

Outside Café, Calver | T: 01433 631 111

Outside Café, Hathersage | T: 01433 651 936
Woodbine Café, Hope | T: 07778 113 882

## Pubs

(See individual routes for recommendations.)

| | |
|---|---|
| Cat and Fiddle | T: 01298 23 364 |
| Cheshire Cheese, Hope | T: 01433 620 330 |
| The Druid Inn, Birchover | T: 01629 650 302 |
| The Fox House Inn | T: 01433 631 708 |
| Ladybower Inn | T: 01433 651 241 |
| The Monsal Head Hotel | T: 01629 640 250 |
| The Red Lion, Litton | T: 01298 871 458 |
| The Royal Hotel, Hayfield | T: 01633 742 721 |

## Accomodation
### Youth Hostels

YHA Youth Hostels can be found in the following
places. For more information please visit
www.yha.org.uk

| | |
|---|---|
| Castleton | T: 0845 371 9628 |
| Crowden | T: 0845 371 9113 |
| Edale | T: 0845 371 9514 |
| Hartington | T: 0845 371 9740 |
| Hathersage | T: 0845 371 9021 |
| Ravenstor | T: 0845 371 9655 |
| Youlgreave | T: 0845 371 9151 |

## Bunkhouses, B&Bs and Hotels

www.peakdistrictonline.co.uk

For specific information, contact a Tourist
Information Centre in the area in which you
intend to stay.

## Camping

(There are many more in the Peak District; search online or call a local Tourist Information Centre.)

**North Lees,** Hathersage     T: **01433 650 838**
**Eric Byne,** Baslow     T: **01246 582 277**

## Weather

www.meto.gov.uk
www.metcheck.com

## Outdoor Shops

**CCC Outdoors** – Hathersage
www.gooutdoors.co.uk     T: **01433 659 870**

**Outside** – Calver
www.outside.co.uk     T: **01433 631 111**

**Outside** – Hathersage
www.outside.co.uk     T: **01433 651 936**

**Jo Royle Outdoor** – Buxton
www.jo-royle.co.uk     T: **01298 25 824**

**The Square** – Hathersage
www.thesquareshop.co.uk     T: **01433 698 109**

**Cotswold Outdoor** – Bakewell
www.cotswoldoutdoor.com   T: **01629 812 231**

**Hitch n Hike** – Bamford
www.hitchnhike.co.uk     T: **01433 651 013**

**Hitch n Hike** – Hope
www.hitchnhike.co.uk     T: **01433 623 331**

## Other Publications

*Day Walks In The Peak District: Book One*
Norman Taylor and Barry Pope,
Vertebrate Publishing –
www.v-publishing.co.uk

*Peak Summits: Eight Classic Walks
(Laminated Map)* Jon Barton, Vertebrate
Publishing – www.v-publishing.co.uk

*Peak District Climbing*
John Coefield & Jon Barton, Vertebrate
Publishing – www.v-publishing.co.uk

*Peak District Bouldering*
Rupert Davies & Jon Barton, Vertebrate
Publishing – www.v-publishing.co.uk

*Cycling in the Peak District: Off-Road Trails &
Quiet Lanes*
Tom Fenton & Jon Barton, Vertebrate Publishing
www.v-publishing.co.uk

*Dark Peak Mountain Biking –True Grit Trails*
Paul Evans & Jon Barton, Vertebrate Publishing
www.v-publishing.co.uk

*White Peak Mountain Biking –The Pure Trails*
Jon Barton, Vertebrate Publishing
www.v-publishing.co.uk

# About the Authors

**Norman Taylor** has been a climber and fell walker since his teens. Since becoming a father with two children in the 1980s he began to plan walks to suit a young family. This resulted in his first publication, *Family Walks in the White Peak*. This spawned a nationwide series for Scarthin Books of Cromford, and Norman himself wrote a further five Family Walks guides. Since leaving the teaching profession and becoming manager of Foothills – the Outdoor Specialists in Sheffield – some years ago, he has been leading weekly, guided walks throughout the Peak District. The two Peak District *Day Walks* guidebooks, published by Vertebrate, are his latest project and are based on an intimate knowledge of the National Park.

To help him in the venture, Norman enlisted friend and walking companion **Barry Pope**. A keen fell walker since his teens, Barry for many years roamed, explored and photographed the landscape of the Peak National Park. In the process, he acquired an enviable knowledge of the natural history and archaeology of the area.

# Vertebrate Publishing

Vertebrate Publishing is one of a new breed of independent publishers, dedicated to producing the very best outdoor leisure titles. We have critically acclaimed and bestselling titles covering a range of leisure activities, including; mountain biking, cycling, rock climbing, hillwalking and others. We are best known for our own titles such as Lake District Mountain Biking and Dark Peak Mountain Biking, which BIKEmagic.com said was *"far and away the best Peak guide we've come across"*.

We also produce many leading outdoor titles for other publishers including the Mountain Leader and Walking Group Leader Schemes (MLTUK) and rock climbing guidebooks for the British Mountaineering Council and the Fell and Rock Climbing Club. For more information about Vertebrate Publishing please visit our website: **www.v–publishing.co.uk** or email us: **info@v–publishing.co.uk**